The Secrets of
Hebrew Words

The Secrets of
Hebrew Words

Rabbi Benjamin Blech

Jason Aronson Inc.
Northvale, New Jersey
London

Production Editor: Bernard F. Horan
Editorial Director: Muriel Jorgensen
Interior Design: Ernie Haim

This book was set in 11/13 Cheltenham
by Multifacit Graphics of Keyport, New Jersey, and
printed and bound by Haddon Craftsmen of Scranton, Pennsylvania

Library of Congress Cataloging-in-Publication Data

Blech, Benjamin.
    The secrets of Hebrew words / Benjamin Blech.
        p.   cm.
    English and Hebrew.
    Includes bibliographical references and index.
    ISBN 0-87668-610-2
    1. Judaism—Essence, genius, nature.   2. Hebrew Language—
Alphabet—Religious aspects—Judaism.   3. Gematria.   4. Bible.
O. T. Pentateuch—Criticism, interpretation, etc.   I. Title.
BM565.B57   1991
296'.014—dc20   90-48735

Manufactured in the United States of America. Jason Aronson Inc. offers books and cas-
settes. For information and catalog write to Jason Aronson Inc., 230 Livingston Street,
Northvale, New Jersey 07647.

The Hebrew word for blessing,
ברכה (berakhah),
has the same numeric total, 227, as the word
זכר (zakhor), remember.
Blessings need to be recalled at all times
and to be always acknowledged.

I am the most blessed of all men
because God has granted me family,
precious beyond words and beloved beyond measure.
It is to them that I dedicate this book.
To my wife, Elaine,
my life's partner and closest friend;
to my daughters, Tamar, Yael, and Jordana;
my sons-in-law Steven Harris,
Stephen Lubofsky, and Aryeh Klein;
my son, Ari;
and my grandchildren,
Avital Shlomit, Eitan Shimon, and Talia Yonit—
the true joys and justification of my existence.

The word משפחתי (mishpaḥati), "my family,"
in gematria is 838.
That is the total of the word וכתבתי (u-khetavti),
"and I have written."
It is because of them—their goading,
their guidance, and their constant good wishes—
that I have been enabled to write this book.

Contents

PART IV

MAN, WOMAN, FAMILY

PART V

BIBLICAL HEROES AND VILLAINS

PART VI

PROPHECIES AND PREDICTIONS

Preface

Hebrew is a holy language.

On the simplest level, its twenty-two letters were used to serve as the language of Torah. It is Hebrew that was used by God to convey His will and His ways, His laws and His insights.

But Hebrew, according to our Sages, not only describes, it also creates. בְּרֵאשִׁית בָּרָא אֱלֹהִים אֵת הַשָּׁמַיִם וְאֵת הָאָרֶץ (Bereshit bara Elohim et ha-shamayim ve-et ha-arez), the first sentence of the Bible, tells us that "In the beginning God created the heavens and the earth." Before the word הַשָּׁמַיִם (ha-shamayim), the heavens, we find the word אֵת (et), which is left untranslated. It comprises both the first and the last letters of the Hebrew alphabet. Indeed, in the beginning, God created the letters, and through the letters and their respective rearrangements, God was able to create the universe.

Scientists speak of matter being formed via the arrangement of molecules. Mystics go a step further. Letters are powers of their own. Their rearrangement gives us insight into the relationship between seemingly different words and concepts. Their numerical significance, their *gematria*, must also be understood, for words that share the same numerical total have a kinship comparable to seemingly unrelated items that share hydrogen, oxygen, or other basic elements.

The Torah, we are taught, is to be analyzed on the basis of four different methods of commentary. They are פְּשַׁט (peshat)—the simple meaning; רֶמֶז (remez)—allusion; דְרוּשׁ (derush)—inference; and סוֹד (sod)—secrets. The first letters of these four approaches combine to form the word פַּרְדֵס (pardes), which means orchard. To study Torah properly is to be placed into a veritable Garden of Eden, finding indescribable delight in an almost infinite number of intellectual pleasures awaiting us.

סוֹד (sod), the study of secrets, beckons to us not only in our perusal of lengthy texts. Words, simple words, used to describe our people or God, life and death, man and woman, biblical heroes and villains, all contain wondrous ideas, which open up to us with but the slightest removal of the "outer covering."

This book is a beginner's text. It is meant to whet the reader's appetite and interest. It is meant to acquaint you with the rewards to be found when taking seriously the talmudic truth that the Torah "speaks in seventy languages" and may be understood on countless levels. If, when you conclude this sampling, you gain deeper love and appreciation for the only language that could have served God's purpose as a vehicle for the message of Sinai, then I will feel more than amply rewarded for my efforts.

A word about the method of transliteration used. We have adopted the Sefardi pronunciation. ח=ḥ. כ=kh. We have not differentiated between א and ע; both have been rendered as a. פ=f. צ=z. Both כ and ק have been transliterated as k (not q for ק). The *sheva* (:) becomes e in Sefardi pronunciation (not i as in the Ashkenazi system). *Zere* (..) likewise is e in adherence to Sefardi custom; not ei as in the Ashkenazi community. Only where the vowel *zere* is followed by the letter *yod*, have we transliterated it as ei. Thus *ben* for בֵּן , but *beit* for בֵּית .

A Note for Readers Who Don't Know Hebrew

You *can* gain a great deal from this book even if you don't (yet) know the Hebrew language.

Fundamental truths of our faith become abundantly clear as we study words for their rich philosophical and spiritual meanings. How we refer to things basically reflects how we comprehend their essence. Shakespeare may have been right: "And yet words are no deeds" [*Henry VIII*]. Nonetheless, they clearly are creeds—beliefs couched in the code of letters merged so as to have meaning on many levels.

Those conversant only with English may be somewhat surprised by the seemingly farfetched inferences, allusions, and even numerical correspondences suggested as credible explications. Yet even English has words that literate people recognize immediately as being composed not simply of letters, but rather serving as acronyms. The word "radar" no longer has periods after each letter to acknowledge its original source, but of course it comes from "Radio Detecting And Ranging." If someone unaware of the story behind the word were to be told that radar can be related to a longer phrase of four words, that too would be farfetched. But ignorance of a word's parents does not justify mocking the parentage once it is revealed.

Hebrew comes with "secrets" far more numerous than the usage of acronyms. The most intriguing, perhaps, and the one often least acceptable to the western mind, simply because of unfamiliarity, is the code of gematria. It may appear as a mere game to take note of the fact that two totally different words, when translated into the language of numbers—for every Hebrew letter also bears a numerical equivalent—share the same total and hence have a relationship. The Hebrew word for child, ילד, for example is 44 (י = 10, ל = 30, ד = 4). Of course, that 44 is the sum of a father, אב (av), 3 (א = 1, ב = 2) and a mother, אם (em), 41 (א = 1, מ = 40).

It is not simply man and woman, sperm and egg, that have merged; it is the numerical essence, the gematria, that is as powerful as genetics in the act of creation.

Gematria is simply a higher reality. When God created the original light of creation, את האור (et ha-or), its essence, not in terms of atoms and molecules, genes or chromosomes, but rather "letter numbers" was 613 (א = 1, ת = 400, ה = 5, א = 1, ו = 6, ר = 200 = 613). That light, as distinguished from sunlight, gave perfect clarity and understanding. So, too, would God later choose to give precisely 613 *mizvot* in His Torah. Equivalence of numbers bespeaks equivalence of meaning.

So, too, shared letters suggest shared meanings. If קבר (kever) means the grave, then how profound indeed that these same letters but slightly rearranged make the word בקר (boker), morning. The concept of immortality finds expression in the very word defining man's final resting place: the grave is but the "morning" of a higher form of existence.

Small children are soon taught that hydrogen, oxygen, and water have something in common. When water is written H_2O, we understand this relationship readily. Gematria teaches us what the "hydrogen" and "oxygen" components of every word really are.

Even Halakhah, the realm of legal categories, acknowledges the validity of numerical meaning. Concerning the *nazir*, the person who takes a vow of consecration unto the Lord to abstain from wine and strong drink, the Torah teaches: "All the days of his vow of Nazariteship, there shall no razor come upon his head; until the days be fulfilled, in which he consecrated himself unto the Lord, he shall be holy" (Numbers 6:5). For how long does a *nazir* remain in this state of holiness? The text simply reads קדש יהיה (kadosh yiyeh). It is the Talmud [*Nazir* 5a] that deduces that the period of Nazariteship is for 30 days. How do we know? "Because the text says יהיה (yiyeh)—and יהיה (yiyeh) in gematria is 30 (י = 10, ה = 5, י = 10, ה = 5)."

What you must know, however, to appreciate the "secrets" of this book are a few basics of Hebrew as they relate to letters:

1. Hebrew is almost always written without vowels. It is only consonants that appear in the Torah; vowels are self-understood in context.

2. For the purpose of gematria, only consonants are included for the numerical count.

3. There are two silent letters, the א and the ע, which receive their sound from accompanying vowels. They are, however, letters with numerical equivalents (א = 1; ע = 70) and they must always be counted when they appear.

4. There are two vowels, the "ō" and "ū," which may appear either as simple dots, in which case they have no numerical equivalent, or together with a ו (the dot over the ו turns it into "ō;" the dot inside the ו renders it "ū"). When the "ō" or "ū" have this ו for "support," the ו is counted as its usual number, that is, 6.

All this sounds far more difficult than it really is. Simply put, every letter that appears in a Hebrew text is also a number. That number is a message.

I promise you that the "secrets" are fascinating. Probe with me beneath the surface and uncover the hidden jewels of the Hebrew language that illuminate the truths of our faith, our values, our people, and our God.

Hebrew Alphabet, Transliterations, and Numerical Values

Hebrew Character	Name	Transliteration	Numerical Value
א	Alef	omit	1
ב, ב	Bet, Vet	*b, v*	2
ג	Gimel	*g*	3
ד	Dalet	*d*	4
ה	He	*h*	5
ו	Vav	*v*	6
ז	Zayin	*z*	7
ח	Ḥet	*ḥ*	8
ט	Tet	*t*	9
י	Yod	*y*	10
כ, כ	Kaf, Khaf	*k, kh*	20
ל	Lamed	*l*	30
מ	Mem	*m*	40
נ	Nun	*n*	50
ס	Samekh	*s*	60
ע	Ayin	omit	70
פ, פ	Pe, Fe	*p, f*	80
צ	Ẓade	*ẓ*	90
ק	Kuf	*k*	100
ר	Resh	*r*	200
שׁ, שׂ	Sin, Shin	*s, sh*	300
ת	Tav	*t*	400

Part I

Israel, God, and Torah

יִשְׂרָאֵל קוּדְשָׁא בְּרִיךְ הוּא
וְאוֹרַיְיתָא חַד הוּא

(Yisrael, kudsha berikh hu ve-oraita ḥad hu)

זוֹהַר, וַיִּקְרָא ע״ג

Israel, God, and Torah Are One

Zohar, Leviticus: 73

Chapter 1
Israel

YiSRaEL

ISRAEL

The Jewish people are descended from the Three Patriarchs—Abraham, Isaac, and Jacob, and the Four Matriarchs—Sarah, Rebecca, Rachel, and Leah.

It is their greatness and holiness that have been transmitted to every one of the "Children of Israel."

The name יִשְׂרָאֵל (YiSRaEL) bears within it the acronym for every one of our spiritual forebears:

י	(yod)	=	יַעֲקֹב, יִצְחָק	(Ya'akov, Yizhak)
שׁ	(shin)	=	שָׂרָה	(Sarah)
ר	(resh)	=	רָחֵל, רִבְקָה	(Rahel, Rivkah)
א	(alef)	=	אַבְרָהָם	(Avraham)
ל	(lamed)	=	לֵאָה	(Leah)

YiSRaEL

ISRAEL

The smallest letter in the Hebrew alphabet is the ׳ (yod).
The largest letter is the ל (lamed).

The very name of the Jewish people, יִשְׂרָאֵל (Yisrael), alludes to both its humble beginnings as well as its glorious destiny:

לֹא מֵרֻבְּכֶם מִכָּל־הָעַמִּים חָשַׁק יְהֹוָה בָּכֶם וַיִּבְחַר

בָּכֶם כִּי־אַתֶּם הַמְעַט מִכָּל־הָעַמִּים

(Lo me-rubkhem mi-kol ha-amim ḥashak Adonay ba-khem
va-yivḥar ba-khem ki atem ha-me'at mi-kol ha-amim)

"The Lord did not set His love upon you nor choose you because you were more in number than any other people for you were the fewest of all peoples."

[Deuteronomy 7:7]

"Yet the smallest in number will be blessed beyond any other and I will make of thee a great nation and I will bless thee and make thy name great" [Genesis 12:2].

That greatness shall come through the very meaning of the letter ל (lamed), to teach. We shall be the teachers of the world, "a kingdom of priests," hastening the arrival of that day when all humankind will proclaim that the Lord is One and His name is One.

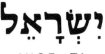

YiSRaEL

ISRAEL

The Ten Commandments were given to the Jewish people on two tablets. All of Jewish law summarized within the Decalogue was divided into two categories: The first five commandments deal with the obligations of man to God, בֵּין אָדָם לַמָּקוֹם (bein adam la-makom), the second five relate to responsibilities of man to fellow man, בֵּין אָדָם לְחַבֵרוֹ (bein adam le-ḥavero).

A religious person is only deemed pious if his concerns embrace both rituals as well as ethics, devotion to the One above as well as decency to man created in His image below.

The Hebrew root for honesty and straightforwardness in human relationships is יָשָׁר (YaShaR). Indeed that is the first part of our description, יִשְׂרָאֵל (YiSRaEL). Add to יָשָׁר (YaShaR) the awareness of God, He whose Hebrew name is אֵל (el), and together we have not only our name but also the succinct statement of our mission.

YiSRaEL

ISRAEL

How were the Jewish people to be counted?

The Torah teaches us כִּי תִשָּׂא אֶת־רֹאשׁ בְּנֵי־יִשְׂרָאֵל (Ki tisa et rosh benei Yisrael) [Exodus 30:12]. The simple translation is usually rendered as "When thou takest the sum of the children of Israel." A more accurate, albeit literal, translation is "When you lift up the head [rosh] of the children of Israel."

We are counted in order to know that we truly count. Because we count, we lift up our heads proudly as the bearers of God's words to humanity, the conveyors of the teachings of Sinai to the world.

A Jew dare not grovel. Mordechai does not bow down to Haman. Within the name יִשְׂרָאֵל (YiSRaEL) are concealed two other words: לִי רֹאשׁ (LY RoSh). I have a head; I have intelligence; upon me is a responsibility imposed upon a people who were רֹאשׁ, the first to willingly take upon themselves the commandments of the Almighty.

YiSRaEL

ISRAEL

אַשְׁרֵי יוֹשְׁבֵי בֵיתֶךָ (ashrei yoshvei veitekha), "Happy are those who dwell in Thy household" [Psalms 84:5]. True joy can only be found in conjunction with closeness to the Creator and acceptance of His will.

The Torah begins with the word בְּרֵאשִׁית (bereshit) and ends with the word יִשְׂרָאֵל (Yisrael). The very first and the very last words of holy writ contain within them this allusion to inner spiritual happiness:

בְּרֵאשִׁית (BeReShiYT) = בַּת (BaT), daughter of (ie., derivative of)

אַשְׁרֵי (AShReY), happiness

יִשְׂרָאֵל (YiSRaEL) = אַשְׁרֵי (AShReY) together with a ל (lamed)—for a יִשְׂרָאֵל (Yisrael) is one who achieves true happiness through the path of לִמוּד (limud), learning and study.

כָּל יִשְׂרָאֵל

KoL YiSRaEL

ALL OF ISRAEL

The Jewish people are divided into three groups:

כֹּהֵן (Kohen) — the Priestly class descended from Aaron

לֵוִי (Levi) — the Levites, descended from the son of Jacob, whose tribe would assist the Priests in the Temple with song and with service

יִשְׂרָאֵל (Yisrael) — the Israelite, the simple Jew

כָּל יִשְׂרָאֵל (Kol Yisrael) means the entirety of the Jewish people. The word כָּל (KoL) is an acronym for כֹּהֵן (Kohen) and לֵוִי (Levi). These two go together. יִשְׂרָאֵל (Yisrael) is a separate word.

Each one has a separate function. All, however, are equally holy. So, too, was Moses always commanded to speak to כָּל יִשְׂרָאֵל (Kol Yisrael), the totality of the Jewish people.

צִבּוּר

ZiBUR

GROUP, CONGREGATION

Jews as a community form a צִבּוּר (zibur), or congregation. A cantor who prays on their behalf is known as the שְׁלִיחַ צִבּוּר (sheliaḥ zibur), the representative of the group.

צִבּוּר (zibur) is an acronym for three types of Jews:

צ (zadei) = צַדִּיקִים (zadikim), the righteous

ב (bet) = בֵּינוֹנִים (beinonim), "the ones in the middle," neither overly righteous nor totally wicked

ו, ר (vav, resh) = וּרְשָׁעִים (u-resha'im), and the wicked

The wicked, too, remain a part of the Jewish people. יִשְׂרָאֵל אַף עַל פִּי שֶׁחָטָא יִשְׂרָאֵל הוּא (Yisrael af al pi she-ḥata Yisrael hu). A Jew, although he has sinned, is still reckoned as Jew.

On the holiest night of the year, as we beseech God for forgiveness on יוֹם כִּפּוּר (Yom Kippur), we preface the words of the opening prayer (Kol Nidrei), with the announcement that אָנוּ מַתִּירִין לְהִתְפַּלֵּל עִם הָעֲבַרְיָנִים (anu matirin le-hitpalel im ha-avaryanim), we render it permissible to pray with transgressors. If we dare to exclude sinners from our midst, how shall we hope that God will consider accepting us with our imperfections?

Chapter 2

God

YHVH

LORD

God is the source of all existence.

הָיָה (hayah) means was.
הֹוֶה (hoveh) means is.
יִהְיֶה (yiheyeh) means will be.

Combining the words for being in past, present, and future gives us the four-letter name of God, by which He is known in the Torah.

It is not, however, simply an allusion to the fact that God *was* long ago, *is* still today, and *will be* unto eternity. In his famous theory of relativity, Einstein taught us that time itself is not absolute; it is merely another dimension, analogous to height, width, and depth. God is יהוה (YHVH) because all three tenses are subsumed by Him; He is the creator of time and unaffected by time. He does not know what will happen "before" things happen—a description that would present us with the problem of predestination and the elimination of man's free will—because He is above the limitation implicit in the word "before" as well as the word "after."

He is יְהֹוָה (YHVH)—occupying all of time simultaneously even as He occupies all of space: מְלֹא כָל הָאָרֶץ כְּבוֹדוֹ (melo khol ha-arez kevodo), the entire universe is filled with His glory.

יְהֹוָה

YHVH

***

LORD

Is God male or female?

A foolish question if we are concerned with physical manifestations of sexuality. Not foolish at all, however, if one recognizes that this name of God ends with the ָ (kamaz) vowel followed by ה (he) which invariably renders a masculine word feminine (compare יֶלֶד [yeled]—boy, יַלְדָה [yaldah]—girl).

This name of God is always used in a context implying מִידַת הָרַחֲמִים (midat ha-rahamim), the Lord showing mercy and kindness in a compassionate role of Mother Creator, even as the very root of the word רַחֲמִים (RaHaMiM), mercy, is רֶחֶם (ReHeM), the womb.

Gloria Steinem thought she was being daringly innovative when she coined the phrase: "Turn to God—She will help you." Judaism long ago acknowledged that God is not only our Father in heaven, but our kind, compassionate, and forgiving Mother as well.

YHVH

❦

LORD

Letters in Hebrew are also numbers. Numbers have special significance.

The four-letter name of God gives us a total of 26:

$$
\begin{array}{lcl}
\text{י (yod)} & = & 10 \\
\text{ה (he)} & = & 5 \\
\text{ו (vav)} & = & 6 \\
\text{ה (he)} & = & 5
\end{array}
$$

From Adam to Noah there were 10 generations, from Noah to Abraham, yet another 10. From the birth of our first Patriarch to the time when the Torah was given on Sinai, another 6 generations appeared on the earth.

For 26 generations the Lord allowed a world to exist without obedience to His will, as an act of compassion from the Lord whose very name is "26." Beyond that, however, His forbearance would not extend; the limits of forgiveness are implicit in the divine name of רַחֲמִים (raḥamim).

ELoHiYM

GOD

We are created "in the image of God." God has a masculine component as well as a feminine one. יִם (iYM, yod plus mem) at the end of a word in Hebrew serves to indicate a masculine plural (compare יֶלֶד [yeled]—boy, יְלָדִים [yeladiYM]—boys; אִישׁ [ish]—man, אֲנָשִׁים [anashiYM]—men).

When God acts in accordance with strict justice, with דִין (din), unswayed by pleas, unmoved by compassion, He is אֱלֹהִים (ELo-HiYM). אֵל (el) is the word for power; its plural is the way that power is manifest in the multiplicity of creation.

As a number, אֱלֹהִים (ELoHiYM) adds up to 86: א (alef) = 1; ל (lamed) = 30; ה (he) = 5; י (yod) = 10; מ (mem) = 40. That is the number identical with the word הַטֶּבַע (ha-teva)—nature: ה (he) = 5; ט (tet) = 9; ב (vet) = 2; ע (ayin) = 70. The laws of nature are constant, cruel, and impersonal. There are indeed times when God chooses to rely solely upon natural law.

ELoHiYM

GOD

The first time God showed His governance of nations in a strict manner was when He destroyed the Egyptians as they pursued the Jewish people at the Red Sea.

The Egyptians deserved to die because of all that they had done to the Jewish people during the years when they enslaved them.

As the Midrash so beautifully states, excessive kindness to the cruel is but another form of cruelty to the righteous.

Divide the name אֱלֹהִים (ELoHiYM) into its two component parts and recognize how the God of justice administered deserved punishment: אֱלֹהִים (ELoHiYM) = אֶל הַיָּם (EL HaYaM), which means "into the sea."

Those who had drowned Jewish babies were now, measure for measure, drowned in water themselves.

שַׁדַּי

ShaDaY

GOD—
THE ALL-SUFFICIENT ONE

If God had created a perfect world, then any efforts on our part to improve it would be nothing short of blasphemous. How dare we build bridges, heal the sick, and enable man to fly? It is because we know that God's name in conjunction with creation is שַׁדַּי (ShaDaY)—a contraction of two words: שֶׁאָמַר דַּי (She-amar Day), He who said enough, stop.

Why did God arrest the Creation before it was complete? To allow man the noble role and responsibility of being "a partner with God in the act of creation."

God tells the first Jew to circumcise himself. It is to mandate a change in the way his own flesh was formed by God.

וַיֹּאמֶר אֵלָיו אֲנִי־אֵל שַׁדַּי הִתְהַלֵּךְ לְפָנַי וֶהְיֵה תָמִים

(Va-yomer elav ani El Shaday hithalekh le-fanai ve-heyeh tamim)

"I am God the Creator who said enough, now walk before Me and become perfect."

[Genesis 17:1]

That verse is the basis of the Covenant and the commandment of circumcision. It teaches that you may, and must, improve upon what God purposely left unfinished.

ISRAEL, GOD, AND TORAH

Alef

FIRST LETTER OF THE HEBREW ALPHABET

א (alef) as a number is 1. It stands for the One of the universe. "Hear, O Israel, the Lord is our God, the Lord is One."

How is the א shaped? There is a י (yod) in the right-hand corner and a י (yod) in the left-hand corner; both are joined by a slanted ו (vav). The י (yod) is 10, the ו (vav) is 6. The total of letters hidden within the א is 26, the number identical with יהוה (YHVH), the name bespeaking the God of compassion and mercy.

We are tempted to assume that the א is a contraction of the longer name for God, אֱלֹהִים (ELoHiYM). Note, therefore, that what appears to be the aspect of God in strict justice is upon deeper analysis actually the Lord of mercy of רַחֲמִים (raḥamim). The א of אֱלֹהִים is the pictorial equivalent and shape of "26."

אֶחָד
EHaD

❧

ONE

The single most important truth of Judaism is the belief in monotheism. Polytheism is rejected—God is not many. The trinity is rejected—God is not three. Dualism is rejected—He is not two. "Hear, O Israel, the Lord is our God, the Lord is One."

The word אֶחָד (EHaD) numerically adds up to 13: א (alef) = 1, ח (het) = 8, ד (dalet) = 4.

His essence is one. His attributes are the 13 qualities of mercy to which we refer on Yom Kippur, the Day of Atonement. They are the 13 *midot*, or qualities, that God revealed to Moses after the sin of the Golden Calf: "The Lord, the Lord God, merciful and gracious, long suffering, and abundant in goodness and truth; keeping mercy unto the thousandth generation, forgiving iniquity and transgression and sin" [Exodus 34:6–7].

EHaD

ONE

God is One. The three letters of the word אֶחָד (EHaD) span across time and the ages in conveying not only God's essence but also the extent of His rulership.

א (alef) = 1 — He began as one alone before time itself, before anything or anyone came into existence.

ח (het) = 8 — The first to acknowledge the Almighty were the Jewish people. It was Abraham, the first Jew, who accepted the covenant of the בְּרִית (berit), circumcision, the mark of the Jew on the 8th day after birth, symbolizing humanity's role to continue perfecting what God purposely left incomplete in His first seven days of creation.

ד (dalet) = 4 — The one God accepted through the covenant of the 8th day will, through the example and the efforts of the Jewish people, become universally recognized to the four corners of the earth.

"And it is said: The Lord will be King over all the world; on that day the Lord will be One and His name will be One" [Zechariah 14:9].

Chapter 3

Torah

TORaH

❧

TORAH

The Torah consists of 613 מִצְווֹת (miẓvot), 613 divine commandments.

Yet the numerical equivalent of TORaH is only 611:

ת (tav)	=	400
ו (vav)	=	6
ר (resh)	=	200
ה (he)	=	5

How can we proclaim תּוֹרָה צִוָּה לָנוּ מֹשֶׁה (Torah ẓivah lanu Mosheh), "Moses commanded to us the Torah," which implies that he gave us 613 laws, if the word itself adds up to a number deficient by 2? Because God, not Moses, spoke the first two commandments directly to the Jewish people: "I am the Lord, your God" and "You shall have no other gods before Me." Only after the Almighty concluded the first two commandments did the Jews, fearing the heavenly Voice, beg Moses to intercede and continue the transmission of the Divine Word.

Moses did indeed command us the sum of תּוֹרָה (TORaH), 611 laws. The other two are in a category all by themselves. The first two commandments are a legacy to us not via the mouth of Moses, but rather from the lips of the Almighty.

ET Ha-OR

THE LIGHT

וַיַּרְא אֱלֹהִים אֶת־הָאוֹר כִּי־טוֹב
(Va-yar Elohim et ha-or ki tov)

"And God saw the light, that it was good."

[Genesis 1:4]

What was the original light of Day One in the week of creation?

It could not have been sunlight. The sun was not created until the Fourth Day. It was a light of far greater intensity. It was a light, according to our Sages, set aside for the future of Messianic fulfillment.

The essence of this primordial light is implicit in its numerical definition:

א (alef)	=	1
ת (tav)	=	400
ה (he)	=	5
א (alef)	=	1
ו (vav)	=	6
ר (resh)	=	200
		613

Light enables us to see with the vision of our eyes. The light of the 613 commandments affords us the vision of insight and the clarity of reality as perceived through the prism of Torah.

ZaHaV

❦

GOLD

The Torah is read publicly on three days of the week. Just as a human being cannot survive without water longer than three days, so, too, the Jewish people cannot survive without the living waters of Torah for that length of time.

We read the portion of the week on the Sabbath, wait a day and publicly read part of the following week's portion on Monday. Two days go by and we are spiritually parched. Thursday refreshes us as we read part of the portion yet again. The eve of Sabbath passes and once more the week is complete. The Sabbath restores our additional soul, and the three special days identified with Torah reading represent the "gold" of our existence.

The letters of זָהָב (ZaHaV), gold, are ז (zayin), 7, ה (he), 5, and ב (bet), 2. Indeed day 7, day 5, and day 2—Sabbath, Thursday, and Monday—are the most valuable of our existence.

בְּרֵאשִׁית

BeREShiYT

IN THE BEGINNING

What justifies the creation of the world?

Without Torah the earth would not survive even for a moment. Because of the Torah God created the heavens and the earth. The first word of the Torah serves as an acronym for the rationale of creation:

בָּראשׁוֹנָה   (Ba-rishonah)

רָאָה   (Ra'ah)

אֱלֹהִים   (Elohim)

שֶׁיְּקַבְּלוּ   (She-yekablu)

יִשְׂרָאֵל   (Yisrael)

תּוֹרָה   (Torah)

"In the beginning, God saw that Israel would accept the Torah."

For that reason and for that reason alone the Almighty proceeded with creation.

בְּרֵאשִׁית

BeREShiYT

IN THE BEGINNING

Why does the Torah begin with the letter ב (bet), the second letter of the Hebrew alphabet, and not with the א (alef)? Because the א (alef) was granted a far nobler and important task. It would begin the Ten Commandments as the opening letter of the word אָנֹכִי (anokhi)—I am the Lord, your God.

The letter ב (bet) is 2. Creation is secondary to the giving of Torah. If ever there were to be a moment that Torah was not studied on the earth, God would turn the universe back again into תֹהוּ וָבֹהוּ (tohu va-vohu), the primordial chaos, or void, that preceded the creation of the world.

חֲמִשָּׁה

HaMiShaH

FIVE

"Who knows five? I know five. Five are the books of the Torah," states the Passover Haggadah.

Torah does not restrict us. It enables us to be free—free to live up to our potential and greatness, free to be more like God in whose image we were created.

The Five Books are meant to allow us to rejoice before the Lord, our God. Their goal is שִׂמְחָה (SiMHaH). Rearrange the letters and see that שִׂמְחָה, which means joy, and חֲמִשָּׁה (HaMiShaH), five, are one and the same.

בְּרִית

BeRiYT

COVENANT

Acceptance of Torah represents our covenant with God.

The word בְּרִית (BeRiYT) means covenant. Yet numerically it does not add up to 613:

$$
\begin{array}{lll}
ב & \text{(bet)} & = \quad 2 \\
ר & \text{(resh)} & = \quad 200 \\
י & \text{(yod)} & = \quad 10 \\
ת & \text{(tav)} & = \quad 400 \\
\end{array}
$$

Why is בְּרִית (BeRiYT) but 612 and not 613? Because the covenant is made with God and presupposes the existence of the Almighty. Although belief in God is implicit in the first of the Ten Commandments, the covenant is possible only after we have already taken the first step of אֱמוּנָה (emunah), faith in the Almighty.

מִצְוָה

MiZVaH

COMMANDMENT

The Hebrew language has two alphabets. One is known as "the revealed," the other "the hidden." The first speaks straightforwardly to us as it moves in logical progression from א (alef) through ת (tav). The second requires the wisdom of retrospect; it is the hidden message of the alphabet in reverse, where ת = א (tav = alef), ש = ב (shin = bet), ר = ג (resh = gimel), and so on.

Every מִצְוָה (MiZVaH) is an aspect of the very essence of God. His sharing of self comes from compassion; מִצְוָה is rooted in the four-letter name of God, יְהוָה (YHVH). The second half of the word (MiZ/VaH) is וה (vav, he), the very last two letters of יְהוָה (YHVH). The first two letters, מצ (mem, zadei), are the substitute letters for י (yod) and ה (he) in the alphabet of retrospect, the one known as the hidden.

Every commandment in the Torah contains within it the seeds of godliness. It begins with reference to the Lord in the language of the mystic and hidden; it concludes with the open and revealed correspondence to God's name. The performance of every commandment may to some extent be rationally explained but bears, in addition, a far more profound significance.

KeTeR

CROWN

Each Torah scroll in the Holy Ark is adorned with a silver crown.

The word for crown, כֶּתֶר (KeTeR), represents a significant number: כ (kaf) = 20, ת (tav) = 400, ר (resh) = 200. The Torah teaches us 613 commandments for the Jewish people. It also makes reference to seven universal laws, the שֶׁבַע מִצְוֹת בְּנֵי נֹחַ (sheva mizvot benei Noah), seven commandments incumbent upon the descendants of Noah.

How significant that the Decalogue, the Ten Commandments under which all other Biblical laws may be subsumed, comprise precisely 620 letters. They, too, serve as a crown for our existence. Pervert them and כֶּתֶר (KeTeR) becomes כָּרֵת (KaReT)—the punishment of extinction biblically foretold for failure to heed the word of God.

מִשְׁנָה

MiShNaH

THE ORAL LAW

The biblical text teaches us "an eye for an eye." The Oral Law or Mishnah, makes clear that what is intended is the payment of money.

The words of the text are incomplete without the clarification offered by oral commentary. The written word of Torah is its body; the explication is its soul.

Rearrange the consonants of the word מִשְׁנָה (MiShNaH) and you have the word נְשָׁמָה (NeShaMaH), which in Hebrew means "soul." When holy men pass away, it is customary to study the Mishnah on their behalf. Let the soul of Torah intercede on behalf of the soul of the righteous, מִשְׁנָה (MiShNaH) for נְשָׁמָה (NeShaMaH).

ISRAEL, GOD, AND TORAH

Part II

The Opposites of Life

הַחַיִּים וְהַמָּוֶת נָתַתִּי לְפָנֶיךָ
הַבְּרָכָה וְהַקְּלָלָה
וּבָחַרְתָּ בַּחַיִּים

(Ha-ḥayyim ve-ha-mavet natati lefanekha,
ha-berakhah ve-ha-kelalah u-vakharta ba-ḥayyim)

דְּבָרִים ל:י"ט

I have set before thee life and death,
the blessing and the curse;
therefore choose life.

Deuteronomy 30:19

Chapter 4
Life and Death

HaYYiM

LIFE

The word for life in Hebrew ends with ים (YiM), the grammatical indicator of plurality. We are granted not one life, but two; not חַי (ḤaY) but חַיִּים (ḤaYYiM).

Why does the Torah begin with the letter ב (bet), which corresponds to the number 2? Because our Sages teach that God created not one world, but two. There is עוֹלָם הַזֶּה (olam ha-zeh), this world, and עוֹלָם הַבָּא (olam ha-ba), the world to come.

Our life must always be lived with the awareness that the grave is not our end, but merely the second beginning. "Know whence you came and to where you are going and before Whom you are destined to give a final accounting" [Ethics of the Fathers 3:1].

חַיִּים

HaYYiM

LIFE

The word for life in Hebrew is written in the plural. When God created the world, He affirmed its innate goodness by reiterating כִּי טוֹב (ki tov), "And it is good" after each day of creation.

Yet when He concluded all of His work in its entirety, He added לֹא טוֹב הֱיוֹת הָאָדָם לְבַדּוֹ (lo tov heyot ha-adam levado)—not only was it not good for Adam to be alone, but the world is not good when anyone is alone. Nothing is satisfying when viewed through two eyes instead of four.

For חַיִּים (hayyim), life, to be true life, it cannot be lived alone.

חַיִּים

HaYYiM

❦

LIFE

Both in Hebrew as well as in English, the word חַיִּים (HaY-YiM) and life each contain four letters.

Central to the English word for existence, surrounded by the first and last letters, is the word "if." Life is subject to imponderables. We are the prey of forces beyond our control, to possibilities both of curse and of blessing.

Central to the word חַיִּים (HaYYiM), the Hebrew word for life, are two י s (YY), which combined form the name of God. Belief in the Almighty replaces the great "if" of life. When God is central to our lives, doubt and despair are replaced by confidence and divine comfort.

HaYYiM

LIFE

Man lives on after death. Not only in the other world, but through what he leaves behind here on earth.

חַיִּים (HaYYiM) in gematria is 68: ח (het) = 8, י (yod) = 10 (2 × 10 = 20), מ (mem) = 40.

Two other words are the exact numerical equivalent of this number: בָּנָיו (BaNaYV), "his children," and וַיִּבֶן (VaYiVeN), "and he built."

ב (bet) = 2, נ (nun) = 50, י (yod) = 10, ו (vav) = 6. His children are his life.

ו (vav) = 6, י (yod) = 10, ב (vet) = 2, ן (nun) = 50. What He built is his legacy.

חַיִּים

HaYYiM

LIFE

The wisest of all men, King Solomon, taught us in the *Book of Proverbs:*

תּוֹרַת חָכָם מְקוֹר חַיִּים

(Torat ḥakham mekor ḥayyim)

"The teaching of the wise is a fountain of life."

[Proverbs 13:14]

The gematria of חַיִּים (HaYYiM) is 68. The source of true life is wisdom. A חָכָם (HaKHaM) numerically is 68: ח (het) = 8, כ (khaf) = 20, מ (mem) = 40. The wise man treasures life. The fool pursues sin and is soon snared by death.

חַיִּים

HaYYiM

LIFE

Jewish law demands that four categories of people give thanks to God for deliverance. The first letter of each category forms the acronym HaYYiM, life.

חוֹלֶה (holeh) — one who is sick and recovers from illness

יָם (yam) — one who crosses the sea and successfully navigates an ocean journey

יוֹצֵא מִבֵּית הָאֲסוּרִים (yoze mi-beit ha-asurim) — one who leaves jail after a term of imprisonment

מִדְבָּר (midbar) — one who crosses a desert and survives

וְכֹל הַחַיִּים יוֹדְךָ סֶלָה (ve-khol ha-hayyim yodukha selah) "And all the living shall praise and thank You, the Almighty." חַיִּים , life, is an acronym for יוֹצֵא , יָם ,חוֹלֶה , and מִדְבָּר (holeh, yam, yoze, midbar).

MaVeT

DEATH

"Why do you weep?" asked the students of the *Ga'on* of Vilna as he lay on his deathbed. "Are you not confident that you will soon be in a world far better than this one?"

"I weep," the Sage answered, "because I go from a world in which with the slightest of effort I can perform מִצְוֹת (miẓvot) to a world where all doors to future perfection are closed for me." מָוֶת (MaVeT), death, in gematria is 446: מ (mem) = 40, ו (vav) = 6, ת (tav) = 400. It is what we remind ourselves of at the Seder table when we partake of מָרוֹר (MaROR), bitter herbs: מ (mem) = 40, ר (resh) = 200 (2 × 200 = 400), ו (vav) = 6.

A Jew must do everything in his power to remain healthy and alive. Live so that you may continue to be able to do the will of God on this earth.

MaVeT

DEATH

מָוֶת (MaVeT), death, in gematria is 446.

That is the number shared by the Hebrew word הָאֱמֶת (Ha-EMeT), the truth: ה (he) = 5, א (alef) = 1, מ (mem) = 40, ת (tav) = 400.

We are all mortal. We cannot escape death. It is the ultimate truth for all humankind. What we must do is prepare for it properly so that we can face our Creator without fear or trepidation.

MeT

❧

DIED

Death atones.

The pain and suffering of final weeks, days, or even moments may play an important part in preparing the soul for its heavenly purification. In retrospect, viewed from back to beginning, the consonants of the word מֵת (MeT) read תָּם (TaM). Through death itself a person may become whole and perfect (TaM).

KeVeR

THE GRAVE

Life ends with the grave.

Rearrange the letters of קֶבֶר (KeVeR) to identify man's final fate: רֶקֶב (ReKeV)—to decay. "You go to a place of dust, worms, and maggots" [Ethics of the Fathers 3:1].

Rearrange the letters again and read the word בֹּקֶר (BoKeR), morning. What appears as night here is but the morning of a higher form of existence. As the Hindu poet Tagore wrote: "Death is putting out the lamp because the dawn has come."

KeVeR

THE GRAVE

The gematria of קֶבֶר (KeVeR) is 302: ק (kof) = 100, ב (vet) = 2, ר (resh) = 200.

It is identical to the number of the words בְּזִכָּרוֹן טוֹב (be-zi-karon tov), "with good remembrances": ב (bet) = 2, ז (zayin) = 7, כ (kaf) = 20, ר (resh) = 200, ו (vav) = 6, נ (nun) = 50, ט (tet) = 9, ו (vav) = 6, ב (vet) = 2.

Death is not final. The soul remains in its spiritual home. The person is recalled here on earth with good remembrances.

Mourners come to the grave to visit, to reflect, and to remember. In remembering, the deceased is kept alive. What we acquire, leaves us at death; what we give away, of our time and possessions, survives us ever more.

חַי

HaY

LIFE

Numerically, חַי (HaY) is 18.

We live truly on those days when we are close to God.

Add up the number of festival days commanded by the Torah: Passover, 7; Shavuot, 1; Rosh Hashanah, 1; Yom Kippur, 1; Sukkot, 7; Shemini Atzeret, 1.

The total of the holy days is 18. They are life on this earth and a foretaste of the life to come.

AVeL

❦

MOURNER

What is the proper response to death?

וַתֵּצֵא אֵשׁ מִלִּפְנֵי יְהֹוָה וַתֹּאכַל אוֹתָם וַיָּמֻתוּ לִפְנֵי יְהֹוָה

(Va-teze esh mi-lifnei Adonay va-tokhal otam va-yamutu lifnei Adonay)

"And there came forth fire from before the Lord and devoured them [*Nadav and Avihu, the sons of Aharon*] and they died before the Lord."

[Leviticus 10:2]

וַיִּדֹּם אַהֲרֹן

(Va-yidam Aharon)

"And Aaron remained silent."

[Leviticus 10:3]

The word for mourner is אָבֵל (AVeL). These are the same letters that form the word אֲבָל (AVaL), "but."

Words do not suffice to deal with the mystery of death. Confronting the unknown, all we can offer is silence. We know that our loved one is gone from us, אֲבָל—but . . . there is more to life than this world. But . . . God has His reasons. But . . . our minds cannot comprehend all that represents the wisdom of the Almighty.

We are consoled by the "but" of reality, which grasps that there is more than the tragedy before our eyes, "but" it is beyond our understanding.

Chapter 5

Truth and Falsehood

EMeT

TRUTH

In English we express the concept of total truth by saying that something is true "from A to Z."

In Hebrew the word for truth is אֱמֶת (EMeT). Its first letter is the very first letter of the Hebrew alphabet, the א (alef). The last letter is ת (tav), the end of the *Alef-Bet*. The exact middle of the 27 letters of the Hebrew alphabet (including final forms) is the מ (mem).

Truth demands total accuracy from start to finish, including every point in the middle as well.

EMeT

TRUTH

From birth to death. That is the ultimate truth of every human being.

The three letters of אֱמֶת (EMeT) may be read in two combinations of beginning and end.

אֵם — Em — Mother

מֵת — Met — Death

From the cradle to the grave—these are the unavoidable boundaries of our human existence. To know this truth is the first step for making the most of ourselves during the time we are granted by the Almighty on this earth.

EMeT

TRUTH

The חֶבְרָה קַדִּישָׁא (hevrah kadisha), the holy society dedicated to caring for the deceased, has its work described as חֶסֶד שֶׁל אֱמֶת (hesed shel emet). It is the loving-kindness of truth, because it is clearly done with no hope for recompense from the person to whom kindness was shown.

אֱמֶת (EMeT) is the granting of three last favors done for another:

א (alef) = אָרוֹן (Aron)—the coffin

מ (mem) = מִטָה (Mitah)—the funeral bed on which the deceased is transported to the grave

ת (tav) = תַּכְרִיכִים (Takhrikhim)—the clothing in which we bury the dead

EMeT

TRUTH

That which is true is everlasting. The false and the wicked cannot prevail.

אֱמֶת (EMeT) in gematria is 441: א (alef) = 1, מ (mem) = 40, ת (tav) = 400.

Man is a duality of both body and soul. Our flesh is mortal. It ages, decays, and withers. But that is not "the truth" of our existence.

וְהַנֶּפֶשׁ (VeHaNeFeSh), and the soul: ו (vav) = 6, ה (he) = 5, נ (nun) = 50, פ (fe) = 80, שׁ (shin) = 300 = 441. And the soul—that is the truth of our life and our immortality.

EMeT

TRUTH

Truth requires for its essence the first letter א (alef), the "One" standing for the Almighty. Remove the initial letter in אֱמֶת (EMeT) and all that remains is מֵת (MeT).

Without God there can be no truth. In its place only death and destruction remain.

אֱמֶת

EMeT

TRUTH

God spoke to us at Sinai and gave us the Ten Commandments, the Decalogue. They begin with the word אָנֹכִי (anokhi), "I am," of which the first letter is א (alef).

The Mishnah, compendium of Oral Law, begins with the word מֵאֵימָתַי (me-ematai)—from when does one read the שְׁמַע (shema) in the evening? The opening letter is מ (mem).

The Gemara, the talmudic discussion of the Mishnah, starts with the word תַּנָּא (tanna), the Sage, with an initial ת (tav).

God makes Himself manifest through His law. In its three forms, Decalogue, Mishnah, and Talmud, its opening letters make the word אֱמֶת (EMeT), as seal of its truth.

THE OPPOSITES OF LIFE

SheKeR

FALSEHOOD

The gematria of שֶׁקֶר (SheKeR) is 600:   שׁ (shin) = 300,   ק
(kof) = 100,   ר (resh) = 200.

To whom does שֶׁקֶר (SheKeR) belong? לָרָשָׁע (LaRaShA), to the
wicked one: ל (lamed) = 30,   ר (resh) = 200,   שׁ (shin) = 300,   ע
(ayin) = 70 = 600.

To the wicked one, falsehood is as necessary as life (חַיִּים
[HaYYiM] = 68) is to the wise (חָכָם [HaKHaM] = 68).

SheKeR

FALSEHOOD

What was the crime of עֲמָלֵק (Amalek), for which they are to be evermore remembered as arch villains?

"Remember what Amalek did unto you by the way as you came forth out of Egypt," אֲשֶׁר קָרְךָ בַּדֶּרֶךְ (asher karkha ba-derekh) [Deuteronomy 25:17–18].

קָרְךָ (KaRKHa) derives from the root word קַר (KaR), cold. Amalek "cooled us off." He doused our passion for God, and by his attack he sought to cool the ardor of our love for God and His commandments.

That, too, is the tragic consequence of שֶׁ קַר—שֶׁקֶר (SheKeR— She KaR), that it cools whatever idealism had been inspired by truth.

SheKeR

FALSEHOOD

Two witnesses once came to undermine the credibility of a talmudic Sage. "We swear," they said, "we saw him rolling on the ground, making wild animal noises, clearly acting like a madman."

What they said was true. They had simply ignored one other vital part of the story. The Rabbi at the time had been playing with his grandchild, happily rolling on the floor with him and imitating both with sound and gesture the wild antics of a goat.

It was a lie not because it wasn't the truth, but because it was only part of the truth. Whereas אֱמֶת (EMeT) covers the entire range of the alphabet, שֶׁקֶר (SheKeR) is a distorted perspective inasmuch as its three letters follow one another toward the very end of the Hebrew alphabet. שׁ , ק , and ר (shin, kof, resh), the Hebrew letters that spell falsehood, afford a truncated, and consequently misleading, view of reality.

SheKeR

FALSEHOOD

The first letter of the word for falsehood is שׁ (shin).

That is the very letter that appears on every מְזוּזָה (mezuzah) as the acronym for שַׁדַּי (ShaDaY), the name of God.

Why does this name of God open with the same letter that begins the word "falsehood" (SheKeR)? Because the power of a lie is in direct proportion to its supposed connection to the holy.

"In the name of God, I tell you this," says the deceiver. At times he or she may even be lying for the sake of a noble end. But the end does not justify the means. The fact that the deceiver has the שׁ (shin) of God in mind does not take away the heinousness of "the big lie."

The Torah teaches: "Justice, justice shalt thou pursue" [Deuteronomy 16:20]. The commentators explain justice—but only by way of justice.

THE OPPOSITES OF LIFE

שֶׁקֶר

SheKeR

❧

FALSEHOOD

Rearrange the letters of שֶׁקֶר (SheKeR) and you have the word קֶשֶׁר (KeSheR).

קֶשֶׁר (KeSheR) is a band, a group, a number of people together.

What gives the lie its awesome power? If enough people repeat something untrue, the world will believe it.

The slanderer in biblical times became leprous. Why did the slanderer, the מוֹצִיא רַע (MOZi RA), become a מְצוֹרָע (MeZORA), a leper? So that he would be isolated. Cut off from others, the liar and the lie can do no more harm.

SheKeR

FALSEHOOD

The letters ק , ר , and שׁ (kof, resh, shin) do not end the Hebrew alphabet. There is yet one more letter that follows.

The ת (tav) is the final letter of truth; it begins the word תּוֹרָה (Torah). The lie may be believed for a while, but in the end truth will prevail.

The giving of the Torah at Sinai was accompanied by the sound of a שׁוֹפָר (shofar) that "waxed louder and louder" [Exodus 19:19].

That is the symbol of truth whose message, though dim at first, becomes ever stronger and louder until it is heard throughout the universe.

Chapter 6
Good and Evil

צַדִּיק, רָשָׁע

ZaDiYK, RaShA

RIGHTEOUS, WICKED

At the Seder we are told to respond to the wicked son: הַקְהֵה אֶת־שִׁנָּיו (hak'heh et shinav), translated as "Remove [knock out] his teeth." The requirement seems both harsh and inexplicable.

The gematria involved gives it a far more profound interpretation. רָשָׁע (RaShA): ר (resh) = 200, ש (shin) = 300, ע (ayin) = 70 = 570. The word שִׁנָּיו (ShiNa[Y]V), his teeth = 366, ש (shin) = 300, נ (nun) = 50, י (yod) = 10, ו (vav) = 6. Take away the power of his teeth, the wickedness concentrated in his mouth. Subtract 366 from 570 and you are left with 204. That is the total of the word צַדִּיק (ZaDiYK), צ (zadei) = 90, ד (dalet) = 4, י (yod) = 10, ק (kof) = 100.

If your child, God forbid, is wicked, a רָשָׁע (rasha), your role and your responsibility is to turn him into a צַדִּיק (zadiyk), a righteous person.

RaShA

WICKED PERSON

רַע (ra) means evil.

What does the wicked person do in order to gain acceptance? He makes central to his very being the appearance of שׁ (shin), the letter appearing on every mezuzah as the acronym for שַׁדַּי (ShaDaY), the name of God. The reprobate will claim that holiness is central to his being. All of his actions are hypocritically assigned to "holy causes."

That is why the father is told at the Seder table, הַקְהֵה אֶת־שִׁנָּיו (hakheh et shinav): the only way to unmask the רָשָׁע (RaShA) is to remove his שׁ (shin), the letter of piety that he uses to disguise his wickedness.

THE OPPOSITES OF LIFE

רָשָׁע

RaShA

WICKED PERSON

How does one explain why someone is wicked?
The Torah cautions us:

וְלֹא תָתוּרוּ אַחֲרֵי לְבַבְכֶם וְאַחֲרֵי עֵינֵיכֶם אֲשֶׁר־אַתֶּם זֹנִים אַחֲרֵיהֶם
(Ve-lo taturu aharei levavkhem ve-aharei eyneikhem asher atem zonim ahareihem)

"And that you go not about after your heart and your own eyes, after which you use to go astray."

[Numbers 15:39]

The eyes ought not to be our rulers. Samson followed his eyes to lust after Philistine women. His punishment, measure for measure, was that he became blind.

Look in retrospect at the רָשָׁע (RaShA) and see that backwards we are told the story behind his aberrant behavior: ע (ayin) the eye, became his שַׂר (SaR), ruler.

A יִשְׂרָאֵל (YiSRaEL) is one who remembers לִי רֹאשׁ (LiY RoSh): I possess a head, a mind, and an intellect that must control the desires stemming from sight. רֹאשׁ (RoSh) also has the consonants שַׂר (SaR), ruler. But central to rule as expressed by the word רֹאשׁ is the letter א (alef), the One of the universe Who dictates the difference between right and wrong, between what my eyes see and desire, and what my head determines is suitable or off limits.

צַדִּיק
ZaDiYK

RIGHTEOUS

When the Jews were counted in the desert, they were asked to give half a shekel.

Why not a whole shekel? Some suggest it was because every Jew had to recognize that he was only half; no Jew is whole unto himself without responsibility to another.

Another interpretation suggests that the Hebrew word for half, מַחֲצִית (mahazit), contains the secret of survival. Central to the word is the letter צ (zadei), the letter signifying "righteous one." The letters close to it and surrounding it are ח (het) and י (yod). Stay near the righteous and you have חַי (HaY), life. Visually, in the word מחצית the letters most distant from the צ (zadei) are the מ (mem) and ת (tav). Keep far from the righteous and the consequence is מֵת (MeT), death.

רַע

Ra

❧

EVIL

There are times when we believe God has inflicted evil upon us.

How do we comprehend wickedness stemming from the Almighty? Moses asked God, "Show me, I pray Thee, Thy glory" [Exodus 33:18]. God responded: "Thou shalt see My back, but My face shall not be seen" [Exodus 33:23]. It is only in retrospect that people can grasp that what appeared to be evil was really meant for some higher purpose. We may curse our bad luck when we miss a plane connection. Hours later, what seemed like ill fortune can be grasped as Heavenly intercession if we discover that the plane we missed, crashed.

At times it takes the perspective of many years to discover that the seemingly bad was but a blessing in disguise. In Hebrew, when רַע (RA) is read backward, then עֵר (ER), we "awaken" to a far more profound understanding.

בָּצַע

BaẒA

UNJUST GAIN

What are the qualifications for judges among the Jewish people?

Jethro, the father-in-law of Moses, made the suggestion that God subsequently approved:

וְאַתָּה תֶחֱזֶה מִכָּל־הָעָם אַנְשֵׁי־חַיִל יִרְאֵי אֱלֹהִים אַנְשֵׁי אֱמֶת שֹׂנְאֵי בָצַע

(Ve-ata tehezeh mi-kol ha-am anshei hayil yirei Elohim anshei emet sonei vaẓa)

"Moreover thou shalt provide out of all the people, such as fear God, men of truth, hating unjust gain."

[Exodus 18:21]

What is the end result of monies gained illegally, of wealth secured through improper means? It is the hindsight of history that shows us that בָּצַע (BaẒA) read backwards is עֶצֶב (EẒeV), "sadness." Corruption gives pleasure for the moment. Theft seems to bring happiness. Yet, ill-gotten gain soon disappears, bringing in its wake nothing but pain and misery.

THE OPPOSITES OF LIFE

YaShaR

"STRAIGHT"/HONEST

Exultation and song are almost always inseparable.

When the Jews viewed the miracle of the destruction of their oppressors and their own salvation at the Red Sea, they sang a Song of Deliverance. אָז יָשִׁיר־מֹשֶׁה וּבְנֵי יִשְׂרָאֵל (az yashir Mosheh u-venei Yisrael) [Exodus 15:1]. The text reads יָשִׁיר (yashir)—not sang, but will sing (the "Y" in yashir indicates the future tense). Throughout the Torah we find nine different occasions when songs of praise were sung. The Prophets tell us that at the time of the Messiah, Moses and the Jewish people will be resurrected. Together they will sing the Final Song and then, of course, י שיר-יָשִׁיר, (yod [10] shir), there will be a tenth song to complete all the times when the Jewish people collectively acknowledge divine intervention on their behalf.

Every act of righteousness today hastens Messianic redemption. Hidden within every deed that is righteous, יָשָׁר(YaShaR), is, through the rearrangement of the same letters, the word שִׁיר (ShiYR). Honesty to fellow man is a song of praise to the Almighty.

PeShA

TRANSGRESSION

Is sin the natural consequence of deprivation?

The very first sin would seem to indicate that the exact opposite is true. It is not because human beings have too little, but rather because they have too much that they are led to disregard divine will and to follow their own desires. Adam and Eve were in paradise, the Garden of Eden. They had but one law to follow.

מִכֹּל עֵץ־הַגָּן אָכֹל תֹּאכֵל: וּמֵעֵץ הַדַּעַת טוֹב וָרָע לֹא תֹאכַל מִמֶּנּוּ

(Mi-kol ez ha-gan akhol tokhel: u-me-ez ha-da'at tov va-ra lo tokhal mimenu)

"Of all the trees in the Garden, thou mayest surely eat. But of the Tree of Knowledge of Good and Evil, thou shalt not eat."
[Genesis 2:16–17]

Paradise, the blessing of having too much, was the cause of our first downfall. Rearrange the letters of פֶּשַׁע (PeShA), rebellious sin, and see the word שֶׁפַע (ShePHA)—overflowing abundance.

Give man too much and he rebels. Give children too much and they become less capable of dealing with their good fortune than if they had been forced to confront life's difficulties.

Chapter 7

Joy and Sorrow

שִׂמְחָה
SiMHaH

HAPPINESS

חֲמִשָׁה מִי יוֹדֵעַ? (hamishah mi yode'a)? At the seder table we ask who knows the significance of the number 5? The answer, of course, is חֲמִשָׁה חוּמְשֵׁי תוֹרָה (hamishah humshei Torah), five are the books of the Torah.

The purpose of divine law is not to restrict us for the purpose of deprivation. It is rather to discipline us so that through self-control we gain true happiness. Hedonism is self-defeating. Excessive gorging leads to sickness, excessive sex to boredom. The purpose of Torah is to help you rejoice before the Lord, your God.

Rearrange the letters חֲמִשָׁה (HaMiShaH) and you find the word שִׂמְחָה (SiMHaH), happiness.

SiMHaH

HAPPINESS

What is the secret for attaining happiness?

Remember every hurt ever done unto you and you will never again be able to smile. Remember every painful experience of your life, and the burden of memory will be oppressive beyond measure.

The Midrash teaches us that God granted Adam and Eve an all-important blessing as they were about to leave the Garden of Eden. "I give you," He said, "the gift of forgetfulness."

שִׂמְחָה (SiMHaH) means שֶׁ (she), that מָחָה (mahah), removed or eradicated, as in the verse from Isaiah:

וּמָחָה אֲדֹנָי יֱהוִֹה דִּמְעָה מֵעַל כָּל־פָּנִים

(U-mahah Adonay Elohim dim'ah me-al kol panim)

"And the Lord, God, will wipe away tears from off all faces."
[Isaiah 25:8]

Everyone has moments of hurt and pain. We differ only in our abilities to either forgive and forget or to forever harbor hatreds and grudges, destroying ourselves in the process.

שָׂמַח

SaMaH

REJOICED

When the Greeks tried to destroy the Jewish religion, they forbade the practice of three laws that they felt contained the essence of Judaic spirituality: שַׁבָּת (Shabbat), the Sabbath; מִילָה (milah), circumcision; and חוֹדֶשׁ (hodesh), the proclamation of the New Moon.

Mattathias and his five sons, against overwhelming odds, overcame this threat to our people. To this day we celebrate their victory on the holiday of Hanukah. And we rejoice because the three letters that form the root of the word שִׂמְחָה (SiMHaH), שמח (S. M. H.), remind us that we continue to be able to practice freely those three commandments for which שָׂמַח (SaMaH) is acronym: שַׁבָּת (Shabbat), מִילָה (Milah), and חוֹדֶשׁ (Hodesh).

שָׂמַח

SaMaH

REJOICED

God did everything for us on the first seven days of creation.

Then, to the first Jew, He gave the commandment of circumcision, to be performed on the 8th day. Its deeper meaning is that man must become a partner with God in the act of creation. We make a change even in the very body that God gave us, to indicate that our role is not one of passive acceptance, but rather creative partnership.

We are the people of the number 8. We must assist and work with God to bring about a better world. Parasites can't be happy. Those who have everything done for them will never know the joy of personal achievement.

We, however, bear the שֵׁם (SheM), the Name, of the letter ח (het), which equals 8, the number implying that we must carry on what God began in the first week of creation. It is that blessing of responsibility and purpose, the שֵׁם "ח" (SheM "Het") that allows us to understand the meaning of the word שָׂמַח (SaMaH), to rejoice and to be happy.

YiSMaH

HE WILL REJOICE

Every Jew has a dream. It is basic to the vision of our Prophets.

There will come a day when the world will be at peace. Nation shall not lift up sword against nation, neither shall they learn the art of war any more. Implements of warfare will be used for productive and peaceful ends; spears will become pruning hooks. God will be universally recognized and all peoples shall stream towards Jerusalem, the city of peace.

That day will be brought about by מָשִׁיחַ (MaShiYaH), the Messiah, or the anointed one. It is his name, its consonants rearranged, that spell יִשְׂמַח (YiSMaH). With the Messiah will come true happiness for the entire world.

צָרָה

ZaRaH

❧

SADNESS

Within every moment of sadness is the seed for even greater happiness.

It was George Bernard Shaw who said: "The desert is a desert because the sun always shines there. Without rain there can be no growth, without storm there can be no creativity."

So, too, did Robert Browning Hamilton profoundly express:

> I walked a mile with sorrow
> And ne'er a word said she;
> But, oh, the things I learned from her
> When sorrow walked with me.

Rearrange the letters of צָרָה (ZaRaH) and you have the word צֹהַר (ZoHaR), a window. Through pain one can see farther, through grief one can gain remarkable vision. The "pain" of suffering can be turned into the "pane" of insight.

Chapter 8

Love and Hatred

אַהֲבָה

AHaVaH

LOVE

What is love?

In gematria it is 13: א (alef) = 1, ה (he) = 5, ב (vet) = 2, ה (he) = 5.

We are commanded:

וְאָהַבְתָּ לְרֵעֲךָ כָּמוֹךָ אֲנִי יְהֹוָה

(Ve-ahavta le-re'akha kamokha ani Adonay)

"Love your neighbor as yourself, I am the Lord."
[Leviticus 19:18]

Two people who love each other become joined through their love. The אַהֲבָה (AHaVaH), 13 of one partner, together with the אַהֲבָה, 13 of the other partner, become 26. אֲנִי יְהֹוָה (ani Adonay), "I am Lord," is the number of God's four-letter name: י (yod) = 10, ה (he) = 5, ו (vav) = 6, ה (he) = 5.

Where man joins his fellow man in love, there God chooses to reside and make His presence felt.

אַהֲבָה

AHaVaH

LOVE

In gematria, love is 13. God demonstrates His love to us through the manifestation of 13 attributes of mercy.

יְהֹוָה יְהֹוָה אֵל רַחוּם וְחַנּוּן אֶרֶךְ אַפַּיִם וְרַב־חֶסֶד וֶאֱמֶת: נֹצֵר חֶסֶד לָאֲלָפִים
נֹשֵׂא עָוֹן וָפֶשַׁע וְחַטָּאָה וְנַקֵּה

(Adonay/Adonay El raḥum ve-ḥanun erekh apayim ve-rav ḥesed ve-emet: Noẓer ḥesed la-alafim nosei avon va-fesha ve-ḥata'ah ve-nakeh)

"The Lord, the Lord God, merciful and gracious, long suffering and abundant in goodness and truth, keeping mercy unto the thousandth generation, forgiving iniquity and transgression and sin."

[Exodus 34:6–7]

We demonstrate our love to Him by accepting responsibility for the performance of commandments upon attaining the age of bar miẓvah, 13. (Girls mature earlier and are responsible at age 12, but the latest number associated with full acceptance is 13.)

The 13 from Him to us, and the 13 from us to Him, combine to make 26, the number defining the essence of the four-letter name, יְהֹוָה (YHVH), the God of compassion, kindness, and mercy.

It is mutual love that explains the reason for His essence.

אַהֲבָה/יִרְאָה

AHaVaH/YiRAH

LOVE/FEAR

Two emotions define our obligations to God in our relationship with the Creator: We must love Him. We must also fear/revere Him and stand in awe of His greatness.

Yet, the two are not separate and distinct. Within love itself there must be a sense of awe and reverence; within fear there must also be an outpouring of love.

Place the two Hebrew letters one on top of the other, in the following fashion: יִרְאָה (YRAH), underneath it אַהֲבָה (AHVH). Draw a line straight down the middle of both words, separating the first two letters of each from the last, as shown below. Note that the יר (Y, R) of the top word may then be combined with the אה (A, H) of the bottom. Similarly, the אה (A, H) of the top word is combined with the בה (V, H) of the bottom. יִרְאָה (YiRAH) and אַהֲבָה (AHaVaH), awe and love, are separate words, but they are also words combined. We love and fear at one and the same time.

$$
\begin{array}{c|c}
\text{YR} & \text{AH} \\
\hline
\text{AH} & \text{VH}
\end{array}
$$

$$
\begin{array}{c|c}
\text{אה} & \text{יר} \\
\hline
\text{בה} & \text{אה}
\end{array}
$$

LOVE AND HATRED

AHaV

LOVE

The three-letter root of אַהֲבָה (AHaVaH) is אהב (A. H. V.).
When does one truly love another?

There are those who say they love chicken. It is not so. If they really loved the chicken, they would not kill it for food. What they intend to say is they love themselves and they use the chicken for self-gratification.

The word "love" ought to be used only as its Hebrew root implies: אֱ הַב (E HAV), I will give.

When I care more about another than I do about myself, when I'm willing to give rather than to take, when the other's happiness means more than my own, then I really love that person.

The love test is simple: Do you want to do more for him/her than you want her/him to do for you?

HiYBaH

LOVE

The word חִיבָּה (HiYBaH) is related to the word חוֹבָה (HOVaH). Love is connected with obligations.

Shakespeare knew it well and wrote in *As You Like It:*

> Good shepherd, tell this youth what 'tis to love.
> It is to be all made of sighs and tears;
> It is to be all made of faith and service.
> (Act V, scene 2)

You do not love if you will not serve. You are not enthralled if you will not be in thrall.

וְאָהַבְתָּ

Ve-AHaVTa

AND YOU SHALL LOVE

We are biblically commanded to love the Lord.

But "how shall I love Thee?" In what way is this emotion to be expressed?

Rearrange the letters of וְאָהַבְתָּ (Ve-AHaVTa) and you find the word הָאָבוֹת (Ha-AVOT), the Fathers. Three Patriarchs begin the story of our people. Three phrases are given to elaborate on the requirement of love toward the Almighty:

בְּכָל לְבָבְךָ (be-khol levavkha), with all your heart. Abraham discovered God in his heart and believed with all of his heart. As the text tells us, "You found his heart faithful before You" (Nehemiah 9:8).

בְּכָל נַפְשְׁךָ (be-khol nafshekha), with all your soul. Isaac was prepared to give up his life on the altar of sacrifice.

וּבְכָל מְאֹדֶךָ (u-ve-khol meodekha), and with all your wealth. As he fled from home, Jacob vowed that if God would protect him on his perilous journey,

וְכֹל אֲשֶׁר תִּתֶּן־לִי עַשֵּׂר אֲעַשְׂרֶנּוּ לָךְ

(Ve-khol asher titen li aser a'asrenu lakh)

"And of all that Thou shalt give me, I will surely give the tenth unto thee."

[Genesis 28:22]

Read the lives of our Three Forefathers and understand the meaning of love as it is to be fulfilled towards God. The paradigms for וְאָהַבְתָּ (ve-ahavta) are הָאָבוֹת (ha-avot).

THE OPPOSITES OF LIFE

LeV

❦

HEART

Hebrew is the oldest of languages.

Some of its words have come almost directly into the English language. לֵב (LeV), heart, became "love." The organ that pumps our very life's blood is associated with what gives our life purpose and meaning.

The very last letter of the Torah, the final letter of the word יִשְׂרָאֵל (Yisrael) is ל (lamed). The first letter of the Torah, beginning the word בְּרֵאשִׁית (Bereshiyt) is ב (bet). Together they make the word לֵב (LeV, heart), for with Torah we find love of God as well as love of fellow man.

But why does this combination appear only if we begin with the last letter of the Torah rather than the first? Because this love can only be fully created after we have completed at least once the Five Books of Moses—and allowed them to complete us.

LOVE AND HATRED

99

אוֹהֵב/אוֹיֵב

OHeV/OYeV

LOVER/ENEMY

There are two words in Hebrew for enemy. One is שׂוֹנֵא (sonei), the other is אוֹיֵב (OYeV).

שׂוֹנֵא (sonei) is almost onomatopoeic; it sounds like what it is. The hissing of the enemy is clear. We are forewarned even as the hiss of the snake announces its poisonous presence.

אוֹיֵב (OYeV) both sounds and appears almost like the word אוֹהֵב (OHeV). It is the word for the enemy who masquerades as a friend, who is, of course, a far more dangerous antagonist.

It was Lincoln who said: "God protect me from my friends. I can take care of my enemies myself."

It was Moses who prayed:

קוּמָה יְהוָה וְיָפֻצוּ אֹיְבֶיךָ וְיָנֻסוּ מְשַׂנְאֶיךָ מִפָּנֶיךָ

(Kumah Adonay ve-yafutzu oyvekha ve-yanusu mesanekha mipanekha)

"Rise up, O Lord, and let Thine enemies be scattered; them that hate Thee will flee before Thee."

[Numbers 10:35]

If the former are scattered, the latter present no threat and will flee of themselves.

THE OPPOSITES OF LIFE

Chapter 9
Peace and War

ShaLOM

PEACE

Jews have 613 commandments. The descendants of Noah are obligated to observe the minimal seven laws of humankind. The seven most fundamental laws are the three for which a Jew is required to give up his life rather than transgress—idolatry, immorality, and murder—as well as four others mnemonically alluded to in the first four letters (alef, bet, gimel, dalet) of the Hebrew alphabet:

א (alef) = אֵבֶר מִן הַחַי (ever min ha-ḥay)—the prohibition against eating flesh from a living thing

ב (bet) = בָּרֵךְ (barekh)—blessing (i.e., cursing) אֶת יְהֹוָה (et Adonay), the name of God

ג (gimel) = גֵּזֶל (gezel)—robbery

ד (dalet) = דִּינִים (dinim)—the establishment of a legal system

Courts are crucial for human survival. Anarchy is suicidal.

שֹׁפְטִים וְשֹׁטְרִים תִּתֶּן־לְךָ בְּכָל־שְׁעָרֶיךָ אֲשֶׁר יְהֹוָה אֱלֹהֶיךָ נֹתֵן לְךָ לִשְׁבָטֶיךָ וְשָׁפְטוּ אֶת־הָעָם מִשְׁפַּט־צֶדֶק

(Shoftim ve-shotrim titen lekha be-khol she'arekha asher Adonay Elohekha noten lekha li-shevatekha ve-shaftu et ha-am mishpat zedek)

"Judges and officers shalt thou make thee in all thy gates which the Lord, thy God, giveth thee, tribe by tribe, and they shall judge the people with righteous judgment."
[Deuteronomy 16:18]

For peace, שָׁלוֹם (ShaLOM), to exist there must be a מוֹשֵׁל (MOSheL), a ruler. The people require discipline imposed by judicial authority. So, too, does every home demand discipline. Only then can there be שָׁלוֹם בַּיִת (shalom bayit), domestic harmony.

ShaLOM

PEACE

The root of שָׁלוֹם (ShaLOM) is שָׁלֵם (ShaLeM)—whole, complete.

Why do people fight against others? Because they are not whole or at peace within themselves. "Love your neighbor as yourself" imposes not one demand, but two, in very specific sequence. First one must love one's self. Only then can one come to love others as well.

Animosity toward others is self-hatred redirected.

Make yourself whole. Find inner peace. You will then come to love your neighbor and be at one with your fellow man.

ShaLeM

WHOLE

For the sake of three things were the Jews redeemed from the land of Egypt.

No matter how low they sank spiritually, they still clung to three all-important aspects of their self-definition and national identity:

שֶׁלֹּא שִׁינוּ אֶת שְׁמָם אֶת לְשׁוֹנָם וְאֶת מַלְבּוּשָׁם

(She-lo shinu et shemam et leshonam ve-et malbusham)

"They did not change their names, neither did they change their language, nor did they change their garments."

[Yalkat Shlomo, Emor 657]

Maintaining identifiable Jewish names; continuing to speak Hebrew; and dressing modestly in traditional garb were the hallmarks of their wholeness.

שָׁלֵם (ShaLeM), to be complete as a person and as a Jew, is to remember what the acronym of these three letters represent: שֵׁם, מַלְבּוּשׁ , לָשׁוֹן (Shem, Lashon, Malbush).

MiLHaMaH

WAR

What is the major reason for conflict? Why do people go to war?

People do not fight because they are wicked. מִלְחָמָה (MiLHa-MaH), war, is waged primarily for the sake of what is central to that word: לֶחֶם (LeHeM), which means bread. Deprived of the basic food staple, wars will be waged for economic reasons.

Help the needy. Feed the starving. Assuage the pain of those who are hungry. It is not simply a commandment. It is the means of preventing war and securing the great blessing of peace.

Part III
The Blessings of Life

שִׂנְאוּ־רָע וְאֶהֱבוּ טוֹב

(Sinu ra ve-ehevu tov)

עָמוֹס ה:ט"ו

Hate the evil and love the good

Amos 5:15

our God,   eloheinu   אֱלֹהֵינוּ

king of   meleh   מֶלֶךְ

the world,   haholum הָעוֹלָם

... Add the ending ...

which fits:

bo·ray   בּוֹרֵא   ha·mo·tzi הַמּוֹצִיא

pree   פְּרִי   le·h   לֶחֶם

hah·aitz, הָעֵץ   m   מִן

          a·ah   הָאָרֶץ.

who creates   gives

fruit.   bread.

bo·ray   בּוֹרֵא   בּוֹרֵא

pree   פְּרִי   הַגָּפֶן.

a·ah·da·ma הָאֲדָמָה   grapes

who create   or wine.

veget bl

Chapter 10

Wealth

עָשִׁיר

AShiYR

A WEALTHY MAN

What is true wealth?

Of course, it is to have your health.

The four letters of עָשִׁיר (AShiYR) teach us what we must have to be wealthy. ע (ayin) is עֵינַיִם (eynayim), שׁ (shin) is שִׁנַיִם (shinayim), י (yod) is יָדַיִם (yadayim), ר (resh) is רַגְלַיִם (raglayim)—eyes to see, teeth to be able to eat and to enjoy our food, hands to touch and to be able to embrace our loved ones, and feet to be able to walk and see the splendor of the world that God has created.

Pray for health, not for wealth.

MaMON

MONEY

Some say money is the root of all evil.

The gematria of the word מָמוֹן (MaMon) teaches us something far different. מ (mem) = 40, twice over is 80, ו (vav) is 6, ן (nun) is 50.

The total, 136, is extremely significant. When Jacob had a dream on the very site that would serve as the place for the building of the Holy Temple, he beheld:

וְהִנֵּה סֻלָּם מֻצָּב אַרְצָה וְרֹאשׁוֹ מַגִּיעַ הַשָּׁמַיְמָה
וְהִנֵּה מַלְאֲכֵי אֱלֹהִים עֹלִים וְיֹרְדִים בּוֹ

(Ve-hineh sulam muzav arzah ve-rosho magi'a ha-shamay-mah ve-hineh malakhei Elohim olim ve-yordim bo)

"...a ladder set up on the earth, and the top of it reached to Heaven; and behold the angels of God ascending and descending on it."

[Genesis 28:12]

Heaven and earth are linked by a סֻלָּם (SULaM). A material object, a ladder, may nevertheless allow us to ascend to the Heavens themselves. סֻלָּם = 136, the same gematria as מָמוֹן, money— ס (samekh) = 60, ו (vav) = 6, ל (lamed) = 30, ם (mem) = 40. Money may be our ladder enabling us to scale the loftiest heights. With money we can build temples for prayer, schools for study, homes for the homeless, hospitals for the sick, shelters for the weary.

THE BLESSINGS OF LIFE

Not for the Jew is the teaching of the New Testament that "It is easier for a camel to pass through the eye of a needle than for a rich man to enter the portals of Heaven." If the wealthy use their gifts wisely, money may serve as the key to the blessings of eternity.

וְנָתְנוּ

Ve-NaTNU

AND THEY SHALL GIVE

וְנָתְנוּ (Ve-NaTNU) speaks of the miẓvah of giving.

The word has a peculiar characteristic. In Hebrew it is a palindrome—it reads backward as it does forward. For to give is not to be diminished, but rather to be enabled once again to give in equal measure.

God gives unto those who assist Him in proper distribution of wealth. When one proves wise enough to distribute of one's wealth to the poor and to charitable institutions, God allows the giver sufficient blessing to give again and again.

         THE BLESSINGS OF LIFE

לֶחֶם
LeHeM

BREAD

When the Jews left Egypt and found themselves in the desert, God granted to them manna, miracle bread, which came every day from the sky.

For forty years, Jews were to learn that daily bread is a gift from the Almighty. It comes from a kind and compassionate God who would later clothe the miraculousness of its divine source in the seemingly natural garb of agricultural law.

Yet we are biblically required to say Grace after every meal, to thank God, since "He gives bread unto all flesh, for His graciousness is everlasting."

לֶחֶם (LeHeM) is 78 in gematria: ל (lamed) = 30, ח (het) = 8, מ (mem) = 40. The God whose name is יְהוָה (YHVH), the gematria of 26, appears through our daily bread three times, morning, afternoon, and night. Three times 26 is the 78 of our daily food staple.

Chapter 11

Wisdom

HoKHMaH

WISDOM

זֶה דְּבַר־יְהֹוָה אֶל־זְרֻבָּבֶל לֵאמֹר לֹא בְחַיִל וְלֹא בְכֹחַ כִּי
אִם־בְּרוּחִי אָמַר יְהֹוָה צְבָאוֹת

(Zeh devar Adonay el Zerubavel lemor lo ve-ḥayil ve-lo ve-koaḥ ki im be-ruḥi amar Adonay ẓevaot)

"This is the word of the Lord unto Zerubavel, saying: Not by might, nor by power, but by My spirit, sayeth the Lord of Hosts."

[Zechariah 4:6]

The world speaks of the right of might. A Jew recognizes the might of right.

The hand is the hand of Esau. Jacob represents the spirit of Torah, and it is the Torah of Jacob that will triumph over the hand of Esau. What is wisdom? To understand that which is implicit in the word חָכְמָה (HoKHMaH). Note the letters within as they rearrange themselves into two words, forming the question כֹּחַ מַה (KoaḤ MaH), what is power?

אֵלֶּה בָרֶכֶב וְאֵלֶּה בַסּוּסִים וַאֲנַחְנוּ בְּשֵׁם־יְהֹוָה אֱלֹהֵינוּ נַזְכִּיר

(Eleh va-rekhev ve-eleh va-sussim ve-anaḥnu be-shem Adonay Eloheinu nazkir)

"Some trust in chariots and some in horses; but we will make mention of the name of the Lord, our God."

[Psalms 20:8]

HoKHMaH

WISDOM

The gematria of the first three letters of the word חָכְמָה (HoKHMaH, wisdom, from the root Ḥ. KH. M.), and the word describing a wise person, חָכָם (ḤaKHaM), is 68: ח (het) = 8, כ (khaf) = 20, מ (mem) = 40.

That, we have learned, is the gematria of the word חַיִּים (ḤaYYiM), life [ח (het) = 8, 2 י 's (yods) = 20, מ (mem) = 40].

Add to life the ה (he), the number 5 corresponding to the Five Books of Moses, and life joined to the Torah gives us the Hebrew word for wisdom.

שֵׂכֶל

SeKHeL

UNDERSTANDING

The wisest of all men, King Solomon, long ago taught us:

שֵׂכֶל־טוֹב יִתֶּן־חֵן

(Sekhel tov yiten ḥen)

"Good understanding giveth grace."
[Proverbs 13:15]

When at the Seder table we speak of the Four Sons, the first is wise, the second wicked. The two descriptions do not seem to belong to the same category. They are not antonyms. The opposite of wise is foolish, the opposite of wicked is righteous. Why are they placed side by side? To illustrate the fact that we believe the wicked person is wicked because he is not wise. Were he but to know better, he would mend his ways. Man does not sin, teaches the Talmud, unless there has entered into him the spirit of foolishness.

Understanding is crucial to piety and proper religious observance. The word שֵׂכֶל (SeKHeL) breaks into two, שֶׁ (She), that, כָּל (KoL), all—understanding is everything.

בִּינָה

BiYNaH

DISCERNMENT

Discernment is the ability to distinguish between things that must be recognized as different. The root of בִּינָה (BiYNaH) is בֵּין (BeYN), which means "between." True knowledge, therefore, requires the ability to observe the difference "between" one thing and another.

Every week at the close of the Sabbath, a Jew is commanded to recite הַבְדָּלָה (havdalah), a prayer "separating" the holy Sabbath from the rest of the week. In four separate blessings, we take note of those four distinctions kept alive by the teachers who founded the Academy at Yavneh in the aftermath of the destruction of the Second Temple. יַבְנֶה (YaVNeH) is acronym for יַיִן (Yayin), wine; בְּשָׂמִים (Besamim), spices; and נֵר (Ner), candle. Havdalah is separation between sacred and profane, between light and darkness, between the Jewish people and the nations, between the Seventh Day and the days of the week.

It is the letters of יַבְנֶה (YaVNeH) that represent the sequence of the הַבְדָּלָה (havdalah) prayer comprising the word בִּינָה (BiYNaH), the gift of discernment granted by God to human beings.

Chapter 12

The Soul

NeShaMaH

SOUL

בְּרֵאשִׁית בָּרָא אֱלֹהִים אֵת הַשָּׁמַיִם וְאֵת הָאָרֶץ

(Bereshit bara Elohim et ha-shamayim ve-et ha-arez.)

"In the beginning God created the heaven and the earth."

[Genesis 1:1]

That duality is mirrored in the creation of man. The earthly portion is the dust from the ground, formed into our material body. Corresponding to the heavens is the breath of God, which infused us with His spirit and allowed us to be created "in His image."

The gematria of נְשָׁמָה (NeShaMaH), the Hebrew word for "soul," is 395: נ (nun) = 50, שׁ (shin) = 300, מ (mem) = 40, ה (he) = 5.

The numerical value of "soul" is identical to the gematria of הַשָּׁמַיִם (ha-shamayim), "heaven": ה (he) = 5, שׁ (shin) = 300, מ (mem) = 40, י (yod) = 10, ם (mem) = 40.

That is why death does not mean extinction. What came from the dust returns to the dust, "for dust you are and to dust you shall return." The soul however, is identical with heaven. It came from God and it returns to spend eternity with its source.

נְשָׁמָה

NeShaMaH

SOUL

Why must the soul be sent down to earth if, as tradition teaches us,

אֱלֹהַי נְשָׁמָה שֶׁנָּתַתָּ בִּי טְהוֹרָה הִיא

(Elohai neshamah she-natata bi tehorah hi)

"My God, the soul Ye placed within me is pure."

[Daily Prayer Book]

What need has it for the long journey of life before it returns to its source?

The answer is contained in the word itself. נְשָׁמָה (NeShaMaH) is שְׁמֹנָה (SheMoNaH), the number 8. It is the number that stands for the covenant of circumcision, the partnership of man and God. In 7 days God created the world and did as much as He would do. Then the Almighty said, "enough" so that humanity could continue the Creation and, through this effort, *earn* a place in eternity.

That task is best fulfilled by studying God's will as transmitted through the Oral Law of the מִשְׁנָה (MiShNaH). Through the מִשְׁנָה (MiShNaH), נְשָׁמָה (NeShaMaH), soul, succeeds in extending God's 7-day creation through שְׁמֹנָה (SheMoNaH) and beyond.

THE BLESSINGS OF LIFE

NeShaMaH

SOUL

Hanukah is the story of the Syrian Greeks' attempt to destroy the soul of our people. Purim was the threat to physical survival when Haman sought to annihilate "every man, woman, and child." In the time of Mattathias and his sons, our enemies wanted to make us forget our Torah and transgress against the laws of our covenant.

The victory of the Jewish people on Purim is commemorated through feasting. Jewish bodies survived and for that our bodies celebrate. Hanukah is the miracle of the survival of the soul. The soul is symbolized by the fire of oil, which burns. The flames of the fire shoot heavenward, defying the very laws of gravity.

נְשָׁמָה (NeShaMaH) is symbolized by a related word that contains its precise letters, הַשֶּׁמֶן (Ha-SheMeN), the oil. Natural law dictated that there was not enough oil to last even for one day. The miracle of our survival is both the miracle of הַשֶּׁמֶן (Ha-SheMeN) and נְשָׁמָה (NeShaMaH), the oil and the soul.

NeShaMaH

SOUL

How do we determine the moment of death?

In the days of the Talmud, we were taught that a feather would be placed under the nose of a dying person. When breathing ceased from the nostrils, the soul had evidently departed. Why? Because life leaves as it originally entered:

וַיִּיצֶר יְהֹוָה אֱלֹהִים אֶת־הָאָדָם עָפָר מִן־הָאֲדָמָה וַיִּפַּח
בְּאַפָּיו נִשְׁמַת חַיִּים וַיְהִי הָאָדָם לְנֶפֶשׁ חַיָּה

(Vay-yizer Adonay Elohim et ha-adam afar min ha-adamah vay-yipaḥ be-apav nishmat ḥayyim va-yehi ha-adam le-nefesh ḥayah)

"Then the Lord, God, formed man of the dust of the ground and breathed into his nostrils the breath of life and man became a living soul."

[Genesis 2:7]

נְשִׁימָה (NeShiYMaH) means breath. The נְשָׁמָה (NeShaMaH) is the נְשִׁימָה (NeShiYMaH) of the יʼ (yod, the abbreviation of God's name, YHVH); in other words, the soul is the breath of God.

Chapter 13

Friends

YeDiYD

BELOVED FRIEND

A handshake is an expression of far more than the meeting of fingers.

With hands we act. When we want to show our love for God, we place phylacteries on our arms to subjugate all that we do to the service of the Almighty.

A true friend is a יְדִיד (YeDiYD)—the word יַד (YaD), hand, repeated twice. יַד (YaD) to יַד (YaD).

The closeness of hands demonstrates the nearness of hearts. One hand is 14: י (yod) = 10, ד (dalet) = 4. Two hands merged in friendship, יְדִיד (YeDiYD) is 28, the numerical equivalent of the Hebrew word for "strength," כֹּחַ (KoaH): כ (kaf) = 20, ח (het) = 8. In friendship there is strength beyond compare.

חָבֵר

HaVeR

❧

FRIEND

The greatest blessing of all is to have a true friend.

חָבֵר (HaVeR) in gematria is 210: ח (ḥet) = 8, ב (vet) = 2, ר (resh) = 200.

Man cannot study Torah alone. It can only be acquired with a companion. With a study partner who sharpens our thinking, questions our insights, and helps to clarify our difficulties, we may come to proper understanding, דֵּעָה נְכוֹנָה (de'ah nekhonah): ד (dalet) = 4, ע (ayin) = 70, ה (he) = 5, נ (nun) = 50, כ (khaf) = 20, ו (vav) = 6, נ (nun) = 50, ה (he) = 5 = 210.

The Torah begins with a large ב (bet). Study it not alone as one, but ב, in two, in partnership with another, so that it will be the source of בְּרָכָה (BeRaKHaH), blessing.

Part IV

Man, Woman, Family

שְׁלֹשָׁה שׁוּתָּפִין הֵן בָּאָדָם
הַקָּבָּ"ה וְאָבִיו וְאִמּוֹ

(Sheloshah shutafin hen ba-adam:
ha-kadosh barukh hu ve-aviv ve-imo)

תַּלְמוּד בַּבְלִי, קִדוּשִׁין ל,ב

There are three partners in man:
The Holy One, blessed be He,
the father, and the mother

Babylonian Talmud, Kiddushin 30b

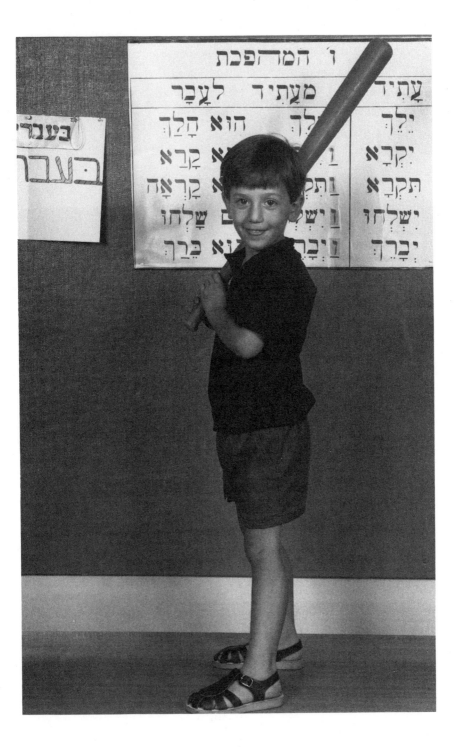

Chapter 14

Man

ADaM

MANKIND

The Talmud teaches that there are three partners to the creation of every human being: mother, father, and the Almighty One.

אָדָם (ADaM) in gematria is 45: א (alef) = 1, ד (dalet) = 4, מ (mem) = 40.

A father, אָב (AV), is 3: א (alef) = 1, ב (vet) = 2. A mother, אֵם (EM), is 41: א (alef) = 1, מ (mem) = 40. Together אָב (AV) and אֵם (EM), 3 and 41, are 44. That still is insufficient for the uniqueness of Adam.

To mother and father must be added one, the One of the universe.

שְׁמַע יִשְׂרָאֵל יְהֹוָה אֱלֹהֵינוּ יְהֹוָה אֶחָד

(Shema Yisrael Adonay Eloheinu Adonay eḥad)

"Hear, O Israel, the Lord is our God, the Lord is One."

Mother, father, and God give us Adam, mankind.

אָדָם

ADaM

ॐ

ADAM

The Torah commands us against consuming blood.

רַק חֲזַק לְבִלְתִּי אֲכֹל הַדָּם כִּי הַדָּם הוּא הַנָּפֶשׁ וְלֹא־תֹאכַל הַנֶּפֶשׁ עִם־הַבָּשָׂר

(Rak ḥazak le-vilti akhol ha-dam ki ha-dam hu ha-nafesh ve-lo tokhal ha-nefesh im ha-basar)

"Only be steadfast in not eating the blood, for the blood is the life and thou shalt not eat the life with the flesh."

[Deuteronomy 12:23]

לֹא תֹאכְלֶנּוּ עַל־הָאָרֶץ תִּשְׁפְּכֶנּוּ כַּמָּיִם

(Lo tokhlenu; al ha-arez tishpekhenu ka-mayim)

"Thou shalt not eat it; thou shalt pour it out upon the earth as water."

[Deuteronomy 12:24]

Living things have blood. That is נֶפֶשׁ (nefesh). But it is not נְשָׁמָה (neshamah), the soul. They have life spirit, but they do not, of course, have a soul that defines the uniqueness of Adam, created in the image of God.

Who is אָדָם (ADaM)? He is דַם (DaM) preceded by the א (alef) and made holy by the One of the universe, who allowed some of Himself to be part of each human being below.

ADaM

ADAM

The first soul created by God and placed into Adam was meant to appear on this earth three different times, transmigrated into three personalities.

The three letters of אָדָם (ADaM), א (alef), ד (dalet), and ם (mem), tell us under what names this soul would appear in the course of history. The א (alef) is Adam himself. The Midrash states that he was destined to live one thousand years, but willingly gave 70 years of his lifespan to King David. In Hebrew ד (dalet) is the second letter of Adam's name and the first of David's name (דָּוִד). The first soul, which might have been perfect but sinned, and which was subsequently perfected through the sweet singer of Israel, King David, would prove worthy to return one last time as the final redeemer. ם (mem) stands for מָשִׁיחַ (mashiaḥ), "Messiah," descendant of David, who will bring the world to universal recognition of God and be instrumental in achieving everlasting peace.

אָדָם

ADaM

❧

ADAM

When God completed creation, the Torah teaches us:

וַיַּרְא אֱלֹהִים אֶת־כָּל־אֲשֶׁר עָשָׂה וְהִנֵּה־טוֹב מְאֹד

(Va-yar Elohim et kol asher asah ve-hineh tov me'od)

"And God saw everything that He had made and behold it was very good."

[Genesis 1:31]

How is it possible that this world, filled as we know it to be with imperfections, could be declared by the Almighty to be perfect? Is human existence as we know it in fact, טוֹב מְאֹד (tov me'od), *very* good?

The answer, of course, is that it is not good from our perspective if we view history progressively, from Adam through David to the Messiah. But if we were only afforded the vision of hindsight, the retroactive perspective given to Moses when he asked to behold the glory of God— "and you shall see My back and My face you shall not see"—we would finally grasp that everything that appeared evil when it occurred was part of a far grander and nobler picture.

In Hebrew, מְאֹד, "very," is made of the same letters (mem, alef, dalet) as אָדָם (ADaM), with the מ (mem) moved from last to first. Indeed, if we could view events beginning with the מ of מָשִׁיחַ (the "m" of the Messiah) and then revert all the way back to Adam through David, we would know that whatever transpired throughout the ages was as God proclaimed it to be, טוֹב מְאֹד (tov me'od), surpassingly good.

אָדָם

ADaM

ADAM/MAN

What is the plural for אָדָם (ADaM)?

The word does not exist in Hebrew. It is to make us aware of the fact that humanity began with but one person. That is why Jewish law warned witnesses in capital crimes to be extremely careful with their testimony, for "one who destroys even one person is as if he destroys an entire world; and one who saves but one person is as if he preserves an entire world."

When we forget the singularity of every human being, that each person is irreplaceable, we take the first step of turning people into numbers, souls into ciphers. Six million victims of the Holocaust are incomprehensible, beyond human imagination. The very immensity of the number diminishes our sensitivity to the tragedy of every single soul. Anne Frank, as one counted teenager with whom we can empathize, makes the crime of the Nazis real and allows the horror to be grasped.

אָדָם (ADaM): every person is one, singular, unique, and can never be replicated.

IYSh

MAN

What makes man different from all life forms that preceded him? א + שׁי —the fact that א (alef), the "One," is (יֵשׁ, YeSh) in him.

In gematria, אִישׁ (ish) is 311: א (alef) = 1, י (yod) = 10, שׁ (shin) = 300. Just as every man has the uniqueness of א, so, too, does every tribe of the Jewish people. שֵׁבֶט (SheVeT), the word for tribe, is שׁ (shin) = 300, ב (vet) = 2, ט (tet) = 9, 311. In every man as well as in every tribe, there is the special greatness of the א, the one God of the universe.

IYSh

MAN

All of existence knows extremes.

יֵשׁ (YeSh), which means "there is," comprises the י (yod), which stands for יְמִין (yemin, "the right") and שׂ (sin), which stands for שְׂמֹאל (semol, "the left").

What is the role of אִישׁ (IYSh)? To place before both of these—the י (yod) of יְמִין (yemin) and the שׂ (sin) of שְׂמֹאל (semol)—the א (alef), the first letter of אֶמְצַע (emza, "the middle").

It was Maimonides, the רַמְבַּ"ם (Rambam), who put into religious categories the Aristotelian principle of "the golden mean." Truth never resides in any extreme to right or left. Neither too much nor too little, neither too full nor too empty, is the way of the Torah in all things, the principle of moderation implicit in every divine commandment.

Chapter 15
Woman

אִישׁ/אִשָּׁה

IYSh / IShaH

MAN/WOMAN

Man and woman share two identical letters: א (alef) and שׁ (shin). אִישׁ (IYSh) has an additional י (yod), אִשָּׁה (IShaH), an extra ה(he). Together they create the presence of יָה (YaH), the name of God, which we constantly praise in the refrain הַלְלוּיָה (HaLeLUYaH).

Without God, all that is left is אֵשׁ (ESh), fire. It is the fire of passion that allows for a sexual relationship, but in the absence of common beliefs and values, fire alone consumes and destroys their union.

אִשָׁה

IShaH

WOMAN

In gematria אִשָׁה (IShaH) is 306: א (alef) = 1, שׁ (shin) = 300, ה (he) = 5.

Every child has two parents. Father is strict; he must be the counterpart to אֱלֹהִים (ELoHiYM), the masculine name of God that implies judgment and accountability. Mother is compassionate and kind. She represents the counterpart to יְהֹוָה (YHVH), which has a feminine grammatical ending.

Honey is often a term of endearment used by husband for wife. דְּבַשׁ (DeVaSh), the Hebrew word for honey, equals 306 as does the Hebrew word for "woman": ד (dalet) = 4, ב (vet) = 2, שׁ (shin) = 300. אִישׁ (IYSh), however, equals 311: א (alef) = 1, י (yod) = 10, שׁ (shin) = 300. The Hebrew word for "man" is identical to the word שֵׁבֶט (SheVeT), the word for the rod and the stick of discipline— שׁ (shin) = 300, ב (vet) = 2, ט (tet) = 9.

We are given two parents. Father must be the disciplinarian. Mother must be like honey. She, like the land of Israel, is the source of "milk and honey."

עֵזֶר

EZeR

HELPMEET

וַיֹּאמֶר יְהֹוָה אֱלֹהִים לֹא־טוֹב הֱיוֹת הָאָדָם לְבַדּוֹ אֶעֱשֶׂה־לּוֹ עֵזֶר כְּנֶגְדּוֹ

(Vay-yomer Adonay Elohim lo tov heyot ha-adam levado e'eseh lo ezer ke-negdo)

"And the Lord, God, said, it is not good that the man should be alone; I will make him a helpmeet for him."

[Genesis 2:18]

Man needs woman for many things. Without her, he is alone. She is to be friend and companion. But it is not only for the present that a woman/wife is a necessity. Without עֵזֶר (EZeR) there is no זֶרַע (ZeRA), without helpmeet there is no progeny, no seed, no children, and no future.

חַוָּה (HaVaH), the first woman, is אֵם כָּל חַי (em kol hay), mother of all living things. If זָכָר (ZaKHaR), male, derives from the same root as the word זְכֹר (ZeKHoR), to remember, woman looks forward, not backward. Her role, more than history, is destiny.

הַצֵּלָע
Ha-ZeLA

THE RIB

The Torah teaches us about the creation of woman:

וַיִּבֶן יְהֹוָה אֱלֹהִים אֶת־הַצֵּלָע אֲשֶׁר־לָקַח מִן־הָאָדָם לְאִשָּׁה וַיְבִאֶהָ אֶל־הָאָדָם.

(Vay-yiven Adonay Elohim et ha-zela asher lakaḥ min ha-adam le-isha va-yevi'eha el ha-adam)

"And the rib which the Lord, God, had taken from the man, made He a woman, and brought her unto the man."
[Genesis 2:22]

"The rib" in Hebrew is הַצֵּלָע (ha-zela). From it God fashioned the first woman, wife unto Adam.

It was woman unto whom was granted "an extra measure of wisdom." She would evermore stand at man's side and be for him לְעֵצָה (Le-EZaH)—the rearranged letters of הַצֵּלָע (Ha-ZeLA)—which means "for advice."

In the words of the Talmud: "If a man's wife be short, let him bend down and incline his ears to listen unto her sage counsel." When in doubt, ask your wife. She was made to give you best advice.

Chapter 16
Family

אָב

AV

❦

FATHER

The first two letters of the Hebrew alphabet are א (alef) and ב (bet).

א (alef) is the one God, ב (bet) as letter stands for בַּיִת (bayit), the house and the home.

Father is the beginning of family life, the א־ב (alef-bet) of what follows. His function is to introduce the oneness of God, the א (alef) into the ב (bet), the בַּיִת , or home.

א and ב together, 1 and 2, make 3. "Who knows three?" we ask at the Seder. Three are the fathers, Abraham, Isaac, and Jacob. Every father must try to incorporate within himself the traits, values, and characteristics of these three paradigms of paternal perfection.

אֵם

E M

❦

MOTHER

The Hebrew word for mother, אֵם (EM), is the same as the word אִם (IM), if.

If the mother is pious, in all probability the children will take after her. The mother is the big "if" of family life. In her hands is the future and fate of her children.

In religious law, a child takes after the identity of his or her mother. For a child to be considered Jewish, it is the maternal genealogy that is primary. As the mother goes, so goes the child. This is why our Sages tell us that at Sinai, God told Moses:

כֹּה תֹאמַר לְבֵית יַעֲקֹב וְתַגֵּיד לִבְנֵי יִשְׂרָאֵל

(Koh tomar le-veit Ya'akov ve-tageid li-venei Yisrael)

"Thus shall you say to the house of Jacob [the women] and tell the children of Israel [the men]."

[Exodus 19:3]

Women are more important than men in religious training. They are to be taught first, for the mother is the "if" of family life.

אֵם

EM

MOTHER

The women of every generation have always been responsible for redemption. In the merit of righteous mothers, we were taken out of Egypt. In the merit of mothers throughout the ages, Jews will be delivered.

Three times in particular stand out when אֵם (EM) served as the word containing the key to redemption.

The exodus from Egypt was accomplished through Aaron and Moses, in Hebrew אַהֲרֹן (Aharon) and מֹשֶׁה (Mosheh). The first letters of their two names, א (alef) and מ (mem), make up the Hebrew word for "mother."

In the days of Haman, the story of Purim came about through the efforts of Esther and Mordecai, in Hebrew, אֶסְתֵּר and מָרְדְּכַי. Their initials, א and מ, too, make the word אֵם (EM), mother.

In the end of days Elijah, or אֵלִיָּהוּ (Eliyahu), will announce the arrival of the Messiah, מָשִׁיחַ (mashiaḥ). The end of history and the final redemption will once again be achieved through the combined efforts of an א (alef) and a מ (mem), indicating the greatness of the maternal idea for our people.

HeRaYON

PREGNANCY

Under the canopy the groom says to the bride:

הֲרֵי אַתְּ מְקֻדֶּשֶׁת לִי, בְּטַבַּעַת זוּ, כְּדַת משֶׁה וְיִשְׂרָאֵל

(Harei at mekudeshet li, be-taba'at zu, ke-dat Mosheh ve-Yisrael)

"Be thou consecrated unto me with this ring according to the laws of Moses and of Israel."

The number of words recited in order to create the bond of matrimony is nine. "Who knows nine? I know nine," we sing at the Seder. Nine are the months of pregnancy. A primary purpose of marriage is to fulfill the commandment, be fruitful and multiply.

הֵרָיוֹן (HeRaYON), pregnancy, is the Hebrew word for this nine-month period. Numerically its component parts are as follows: ה (he) = 5, ר (resh) = 200, י (yod) = 10, ו (vav) = 6, ן (nun) = 50. Pregnancy in gematria is 271, the exact number of days required for the fetus to develop fully within the womb of its mother.

בֵּן

BeN

SON

Jewish law decrees that a child assumes the religious identity of his or her mother.

A child is Jewish when the mother is Jewish. If the mother is a non-Jewess, so is her offspring.

The two letters making up the word for "son," ב (bet) and נ (nun), follow in the Hebrew alphabet the letters א (alef) and מ (mem).

The word itself teaches us that בֵּן follows אֵם, the child takes after the mother.

BaT

DAUGHTER

It is the daughter, the בַּת (BaT), whose special responsibility is to build the spirituality of the בַּיִת (BaYiT), the home.

The very first letter of the Torah is the ב (bet), written large to indicate that Torah comes primarily from the home. Jewish families are created not in synagogues or temples, but rather in the close-knit sanctuary of the household.

When the בַּת (bat), the daughter, makes central to her very being the י (yod) of יְהֹוָה (YHVH), four walls are turned into a temple and the future is assured.

אָח

A Ḥ

🙬

BROTHER

Adam and Eve were, of course, husband and wife.

Yet, the first letters of אָדָם (Adam) and חַוָּה (Ḥavah), the original Hebrew names, together make the word אָח (AḤ).

Their union was not simply sexual. They were like brother and sister. They enjoyed friendship and fellowship.

At a wedding ceremony we say שַׂמֵחַ תְּשַׂמַּח רֵעִים אֲהוּבִים (same'aḥ tesamaḥ re'im ahuvim), "make the bride and groom rejoice as friends and lovers"—friends first and then lovers. How great is sexual union founded on mutual love and respect.

נִידָה

NiYDaH

THE MENSTRUATING WOMAN

In Judaism, celibacy is sinful. Whatever God created is good. To deny oneself totally of God's blessings is to proclaim evil what God has called good.

Yet, there are limits imposed upon us with regard to sexual pleasure. A woman during the time of her period is sexually off limits to her husband so that when they reunite, it will be as if they once again come together as at the time of their honeymoon.

נִידָה (NiYDaH) is nothing other than דִין (DiYN), the law of ה (he)— יְהֹוָה, the God of compassion and mercy, Who proclaims laws which, when understood, are in our own best interests.

Part V
Biblical Heroes
and Villains

כִּי כִשְׁמוֹ כֶּן־הוּא
(Ki khi-shemo ken hu)

שְׁמוּאֵל א׳ כ״ה:כ״ה

For as his name is, so is he

First Samuel 25:25

Chapter 17

The Heroes

נֹחַ

NoaH

❦

NOAH

נֹחַ אִישׁ צַדִּיק תָּמִים הָיָה בְּדֹרֹתָיו אֶת־הָאֱלֹהִים הִתְהַלֶּךְ־נֹחַ

(Noaḥ ish ẓadiyk tamim hayah be-dorotav et ha-Elohim hitha-lekh Noaḥ)

"Noah was in his generations a man righteous and whole-hearted; Noah walked with God."

[Genesis 6:9]

Yet, Noah was not the first Jew. It remained for Abraham to become the Patriarch of our people.

In what way was Abraham superior to Noah? Are we not told that Noah "walked with God?" Abraham, too, loved God, but when he stood speaking to the Almighty and saw three strangers approaching, Abraham left the divine presence to take care of the more pressing need of starving strangers. For Noah, however, it was more important to find favor in the eyes of God than in the eyes of man—which is why he could ignore an entire world doomed to destruction and be content to find salvation in "his own little ark." Noah had it all backwards. He "found favor" in reverse, which is why the name נֹחַ (NoaH) reads חֵן (HeN), finding favor, only when it is read from left to right, instead of right to left. Noah was not the first Jew, because he had his priorities backwards.

נֹחַ

NoaH

❧

NOAH

Noah was the first inventor. Noah lived in an age of corruption that had to be destroyed by the flood for its wickedness. And the two were not unconnected.

Noah invented the plow. The name נֹחַ is related to נָח (NaH), which means "rest." For the first time, people did not have to work so very hard in order to produce food from the ground. Noah gave a measure of rest to the world.

What happens when people have too much free time on their hands? In their inability to use this new-found time creatively and productively, people became immoral and depraved.

It was the age of Noah, of "rest," that is known as the generation of the flood.

AVRaHaM

ABRAHAM

The 613 commandments of the Torah are divided into 248 positive commandments and 365 negative ones.

The 248 positive commandments correspond to the organs in the body, every one of which is identified with a corresponding miẓvah. The 365 negative commandments correspond to the solar days of the year.

אַבְרָהָם (AVRaHaM), the first Jew, is the paradigm of perfection with regard to fulfillment of God's will. The gematria of his name has a specific meaning: א (alef) = 1, ב (vet) = 2, ר (resh) = 200, ה (he) = 5, מ (mem) = 40. The total is 248, the number of positive commandments.

Even before Sinai, Abraham intuitively grasped the positive commandments and fulfilled them. Every organ of his body strove to actualize the potential implicit in it, so that working in concert, the organs of his entire body proclaimed the greatness of God.

AVRaHaM

ABRAHAM

God created the world only for the sake of the righteous who would inhabit it.

זֶה סֵפֶר תּוֹלְדֹת אָדָם בְּיוֹם בְּרֹא אֱלֹהִים אָדָם בִּדְמוּת אֱלֹהִים עָשָׂה אֹתוֹ׃
זָכָר וּנְקֵבָה בְּרָאָם וַיְבָרֶךְ אֹתָם וַיִּקְרָא אֶת־שְׁמָם אָדָם בְּיוֹם הִבָּרְאָם׃

(Zeh sefer toledot adam be-yom bero Elohim adam bi-demut Elohim asah oto. Zakhar u-nekevah bera'am va-yevarekh otam vay-yikra et shemam Adam be-yom hi-baram)

"This is the book of the generations of Adam. In the day that God created man, in the likeness of God made He him; male and female created He them, and blessed them, and called their name Adam, in the day when they were created."

[Genesis 5:1-2]

הִבָּרְאָם (HiBaRAM), they were created—Adam and Eve, the progenitors of the human race—for the sake of those very letters in הִבָּרְאָם . Rearrange them and you find the name אַבְרָהָם (AVRa-HaM), Abraham.

YiZHaK

ISAAC

The two children of Abraham would each be ancestors of different peoples. They would represent two totally different cultures, at war with the other to this very day. Isaac fathers Jacob, and we are the children of Israel. Ishmael is the ancestor of all the Arab nations.

Isaac is יִצְחָק (YiZHaK)—"he will laugh." Ishmael was rejected by Sarah and cast out of the household because

וַתֵּרֶא שָׂרָה אֶת־בֶּן־הָגָר הַמִּצְרִית אֲשֶׁר־יָלְדָה לְאַבְרָהָם מְצַחֵק:

(Va-tere Sarah et ben Hagar ha-miẓrit asher yaldah le-Avraham meẓaḥek)

"And Sarah saw the son of Hagar, the Egyptian, whom she had born unto Abraham making sport."

[Genesis 21:9]

What is the crucial difference between יִצְחָק (YiZHaK) and the one who is מְצַחֵק (MeZaHeK)? מְצַחֵק (MeZaHeK) is laughter in the present tense. It is an outlook that demands immediate gratification. It is identified by the Midrash with sexual immorality, bloodshed, and idolatry. יִצְחָק (YiZHaK), prefaced by the י (yod) that turns the root into the future tense, is willing to defer laughter. The world to come is more valuable and longed for than the present time. יִצְחָק (YiZHaK, or Isaac) can say no to the here and now for the sake of eternity.

יִצְחָק (YiZHaK) will laugh—and he who laughs last, laughs best.

יִצְחָק

YiZHaK

ISAAC

Four letters define the son of Abraham the Patriarch and allude to his greatness.

 י (yod) — 10, referring to the Ten Commandments

צ (zadei) — 90, the age of Sarah at which she miraculously bore Isaac

ח (het) — 8, the day when Isaac was circumcised and given his name יִצְחָק (YiZHaK)

ק (kof) — 100, the age of Abraham, his father, at the time when he sired him

A miracle performed for a mother and father, respectively aged 90 and 100, was for the sake of a child who would be circumcised and enter a covenant subsequently defined at Sinai through the Ten Commandments.

יַעֲקֹב

Ya'AKoV

JACOB

The genetic impurities of the first two Patriarchs were successfully uprooted in Jacob's progeny. Abraham had Isaac and Ishmael. Isaac had Jacob and Esau.

Jacob's children were all pure and holy. יַעֲקֹב (Ya'AKoV) is talmudically referred to as בְּחִיר הָאָבוֹת (beḥir ha-avot), the chosen of the ancestors.

In gematria, יַעֲקֹב is י (yod) = 10, ע (ayin) = 70, ק (kof) = 100, ב (vet) = 2, which is 182.

That, says the Midrash, is the equivalent of the two words מַלְאַךְ הָאֱלֹהִים (MaLAKH Ha ELoHiYM), angel of God. מ (mem) = 40, ל (lamed) = 30, א (alef) = 1, ךְ (khaf) = 20, ה (he) = 5, א (alef) = 1, ל (lamed) = 30, ה (he) = 5, י (yod) = 10, ם (mem) = 40.

Ya'AKoV

JACOB

The world rests on three foundations, we are taught in *Ethics of the Fathers:* תּוֹרָה (Torah), עֲבוֹדָה (avodah), and גְּמִילוּת חֲסָדִים (gemilut ḥasadim)—Torah, sacrifice, and acts of lovingkindness.

Each one of our Patriarchs specialized in bringing to perfection one of these three traits. Abraham epitomized kindness to others. Isaac was ready to offer himself as a sacrifice. Jacob sat in the tent and dedicated his life to the study of Torah.

Jacob's Hebrew name, יַעֲקֹב (Ya'AKoV), contains the י (yod) of the Ten Commandments followed by עֲקֹב , ע (ayin) = 70, ק (kof) = 100, ב (vet) = 2, the total 172 being exactly the number of words that appear in the Decalogue.

אַבְרָהָם, יִצְחָק, יַעֲקֹב

AVRaHaM, YiZHaK, Ya'AKoV

ABRAHAM, ISAAC, JACOB

A Jew prays three times a day.

The three daily prayers—the morning service, the afternoon service, and the evening service—were each instituted by one of our Patriarchs. It is the second letters of their names that reveal the time of day they sanctified when communicating with God.

(Avraham = **B**oker)	אַ**בְ**רָהָם	=	בּוֹקֶר /morning
(Yizhak = **Z**ohorayim)	יִ**צְ**חָק	=	צָהֳרַיִם /midday
(Ya'akov = **E**rev)	יַ**עֲ**קֹב	=	עֶרֶב /evening

These are not simply three moments, but three moods as well. In the morning, as the sun rises, we are blessed; in the afternoon, as the sun begins to sink, we fear for our good fortune; and in the darkness of night we sense its great potential for danger. Whatever our lot in life may be, we acknowledge that God knows what is best for us and we must be both grateful and accepting.

YeHUDaH

JUDAH

Of the twelve sons of Jacob, Judah would be the one destined to become the ancestor of the Davidic dynasty as well as the Messiah.

The role of the Messiah is to bring about the universal recognition of God. Within the name יְהוּדָה (YeHUDaH) we find the four-letter name of God, יְהֹוָה (YHVH), together with a ד (dalet). ד (dalet) is 4 because it would be the task of the seed of Judah to make the nations in the four corners of the world acknowledge the four-letter name of God.

MoSheH

MOSES

What made Moses the greatest of all men? Why did God select him as the leader of our people?

The Midrash relates that when Moses was a shepherd, he brought his flock to the water. One day, one little lamb did not come to drink. When Moses saw the lost lamb, he felt compassion and carried it in his own hands to the stream.

Moses cared not simply for the large group under his control, but for every single one. And like the Almighty, "His mercy extended over all His works."

Read מֹשֶׁה (MoSheH), Moses' Hebrew name, as two words— מ (Mi), from, שֶׂה (SeH), the lamb—the little lamb that proved the extent of his feeling and concern for others.

מֹשֶׁה

MoSheH

MOSES

Moses was great, but he was not a god.
The very chapter that introduces his birth tells us

וַיֵּלֶךְ אִישׁ מִבֵּית לֵוִי וַיִּקַּח אֶת־בַּת־לֵוִי: וַתַּהַר הָאִשָּׁה וַתֵּלֶד בֵּן

(Va-yelekh ish mi-beit levi vay-yikaḥ et bat levi. Va-tahar ha-
ishah va-teled ben)

"And there went a *man* of the house of Levi and he took to
wife a daughter of Levi and the woman conceived and bore a
son."

[Exodus 2:1–2]

He was not born of the gods, but from human parentage; his
mother was not a virgin, but she conceived in a normal manner.
So, too, would his very burial site remain hidden forever so that it
would not become a place of excessive veneration or deification.
The gematria of מֹשֶׁה (MoSheH) is 345: מ (mem) = 40, ש
(shin) = 300, ה (he) = 5. The very first time that number appears in
a word in the Torah is in Genesis 6:3:

וַיֹּאמֶר יְהֹוָה לֹא־יָדוֹן רוּחִי בָאָדָם לְעֹלָם בְּשַׁגַּם הוּא
בָשָׂר וְהָיוּ יָמָיו מֵאָה וְעֶשְׂרִים שָׁנָה

(Va-yomer Adonay lo yadon ruḥi va-adam le-olam be-shagam
hu vasar ve-hayu yamav me'ah ve-esrim shanah)

"And the Lord said my spirit shall not abide in man forever
for that he also is flesh; therefore shall his days be 120 years."

The word בְּשַׁגַּם (BeShaGaM), "for," is 345: ב (bet) = 2, שׁ (shin) = 300, ג (gimel) = 3, מ (mem) = 40. Indeed, Moses was granted long life, but he lived only until 120—and that remains the most longed for blessing amongst our people: May you live to the age of מֹשֶׁה (MoSheH), until 120.

מֹשֶׁה

MoSheH

✿

MOSES

In order to accept God and Torah, one must first do away with the idolatries of one's time.

Before the Jews in Egypt could commit themselves to God's will at Sinai, they had to indicate their willingness to slaughter the strongest god of Egypt. Since the lamb was an object of worship, the Jews were obligated not only to bring it as a paschal offering, but also to publicly proclaim their action by smearing its blood on the doorpost of their home. Only when God would see this public display of faith would He "pass over" Jewish homes and spare their inhabitants.

That was the first message Moses was told to convey to the Jewish people.

דַּבְּרוּ אֶל־כָּל־עֲדַת יִשְׂרָאֵל לֵאמֹר בֶּעָשֹׂר לַחֹדֶשׁ הַזֶּה וְיִקְחוּ
לָהֶם אִישׁ שֶׂה לְבֵית־אָבֹת שֶׂה לַבָּיִת

(Dabru el kol adat Yisrael lemor be-asor la-hodesh ha-zeh ve-yikhu lahem ish seh le-veit avot seh la-bayit)

"Speak ye unto all the congregation of Israel saying: In the tenth day of this month they shall take to them every man a lamb, according to their fathers' houses, a lamb for a household."

[Exodus 12:3]

A lamb is a שֶׂה (SeH), and מֹשֶׁה (MoSheH) Moses was to wean the Jewish people "away," מ (Mi), from, שֶׂה (SeH), this lamb of Egyptian worship.

MoSheH

MOSES

In retrospect, what was the role of מֹשֶה (MoSheH)?

Read his name backwards and understand: הַשֵם (HaSheM), the Name, the term used to describe the Almighty, would become manifest through him.

Moses was merely the medium. He was the scribe; God was the author. Moses "wrote" the Torah as much as a secretary may be said to have written the works of a prominent author.

We must respect and revere Moses, the man. On Passover night we do not mention him by name even once, in order to prevent the glorification of the messenger above the message—or the One who sent him.

מֹשֶׁה רַבֵּינוּ

MoSheH RaBeYNU

MOSES OUR TEACHER

Find the total of the words מֹשֶׁה רַבֵּינוּ (MoSheH RaBeYNU), Moses our teacher, and note an obvious message. מֹשֶׁה equals מ (mem) = 40, שׁ (shin) = 300, ה (he) = 5, or 345; רַבֵּינוּ equals ר (resh) = 200, ב (bet) = 2, י (yod) = 10, נ (nun) = 50, ו (vav) = 6 or 268. Together, 345 + 268 = 613. There are 613 commandments in the Torah, and Moses our teacher was the one who made them known unto us in the Five Books of Moses.

AHaRoN

AARON

Moses brought us the law. Aaron was in charge of the Temple.

Law had to be brought to the people, and Aaron's personality was such that he was

אוֹהֵב שָׁלוֹם וְרוֹדֵף שָׁלוֹם, אוֹהֵב אֶת הַבְּרִיּוֹת וּמְקַרְבָן לַתּוֹרָה

(Ohev shalom ve-rodef shalom, ohev et ha-beriyot u-mekar-van la-Torah)

"One who loves peace and pursues peace, loves mankind and draws them near to Torah."

[Ethics of the Fathers 1:12]

Aaron was ideally suited to be High Priest. He was in charge of the מִשְׁכָּן (mishkan), the Tabernacle, whose purpose was clearly set forth:

וְעָשׂוּ לִי מִקְדָּשׁ וְשָׁכַנְתִּי בְּתוֹכָם

(Ve-asu li mikdash ve-shakhanti be-tokham)

"And let them make me a sanctuary that I may dwell among them."

[Exodus 25:8]

The focal point of the sanctuary was the ark in which the Tablets were kept. The ark in Hebrew is הָאָרֹן (Ha-ARoN). Note that the letters of the foremost item in the sanctuary rearrange to make the word אַהֲרֹן (AHaRoN).

רות

RUT

RUTH

Ruth came to the Jewish people of her own volition.

The book named after her is read on Shavuot, the festival of the giving of the Torah. The Torah was given in the desert, not in the land of Israel, because it was meant not simply for the Jewish people but for humanity as a whole. The Jews were not so much the Chosen People as the choosing people. When all other nations refused God's offer to accept the Torah, the Jews proclaimed "we will do and we will listen."

Ruth is a convert who paves the way for others. Eventually, her descendant, King David, serves as ancestor of the Messiah, who will bring the entire world to the recognition that Ruth demonstrated in her own life when she said, "Your people is my people, your God is my God."

Her name, רות (RUT), is in fact the key to her greatness. Born a non-Jew, she was responsible only for the Seven Universal Laws. רות (RUT) in gematria is 606: ר (resh) = 200, ו (vav) = 6, ת (tav) = 400. She desired not simply the Seven Universal Laws but all 613, and so רות (RUT) took upon herself the additional 606. Her name reflects that number of divine commandments that she voluntarily and joyfully added to her commitment.

MaShiYaH

MESSIAH

It is the vision of the Messianic era to which we allude at the close of every prayer service.

At the conclusion of the עָלֵינוּ (Aleinu), the closing prayer, we recite:

וְנֶאֱמַר: וְהָיָה יְהֹוָה לְמֶלֶךְ עַל־כָּל־הָאָרֶץ,
בַּיּוֹם הַהוּא יִהְיֶה יְהֹוָה אֶחָד וּשְׁמוֹ אֶחָד

(Ve-ne'emar: Ve-hayah Adonay le-melekh al kol ha-arez, ba-yom ha-hu yihyeh Adonay eḥad u-shemo eḥad)

"And it is said God will be King over all the world—on that day God will be One and His name will be One."

[Zechariah: 14:9]

מָשִׁיחַ (MaShiYaH) means the anointing one. Read backwards, the name tells us what he will achieve— חַי (HaY), there will then live, שֵׁם (SheM), the name of the Almighty.

MaShiYaH

MESSIAH

The gematria of מָשִׁיחַ (MaShiYaH) is 358: מ (mem) = 40, שׁ (shin) = 300, ' (yod) = 10, ח (het) = 8.

When the children of Jacob came down to Egypt, they understood that they could not live together with the Egyptians in the same areas. Closeness would lead to intermarriage and assimilation.

It was the children of Israel who created the first ghetto—a voluntary ghetto not imposed from without, but voluntarily decided upon from within.

וְאֶת־יְהוּדָה שָׁלַח לְפָנָיו אֶל־יוֹסֵף לְהוֹרֹת לְפָנָיו גֹּשְׁנָה וַיָּבֹאוּ אַרְצָה גֹּשֶׁן:

(Ve-et Yehudah shalah le-fanav el Yosef le-horot le-fanav Goshnah va-yavo'u arẓah Goshen)

"And Judah sent before Him unto Joseph to show the way before him unto Goshen; and they came into the land of Goshen."

[Genesis 46:28]

גֹּשְׁנָה (GoShNaH) is the secret of Jewish survival. ג (gimel) = 3, שׁ (shin) = 300, נ (nun) = 50, ה (he) = 5, a total of 358. Because of גֹּשְׁנָה , our self-imposed separatism, we will be privileged to witness the coming of the Messiah, מָשִׁיחַ (MaShiYaH), which also equals 358.

Chapter 18
The Villains

KaYiN

❦

CAIN

Cain was the first murderer in all of human history.

His name bespeaks a terrible error in judgment on the part of his mother, who named him. In Hebrew, there is a correlation between Cain's name—KaYiN—and the verb "to acquire," KaNiYTiY.

וְהָאָדָם יָדַע אֶת־חַוָּה אִשְׁתּוֹ וַתַּהַר וַתֵּלֶד אֶת־קַיִן
וַתֹּאמֶר קָנִיתִי אִישׁ אֶת־יְהֹוָה:

(Ve-ha-Adam yada et Havah ishto va-tahar va-teled et Kayin va-tomer Kaniti ish et Adonay)

"And the man knew Eve his wife and she conceived and bore Cain and said, I have acquired a man with the help of the Lord."

[Genesis 4:1]

No person is ever to be "acquired" by another. Even a child does not "belong" to his parents. A child is a person, not an object; a human being, not a thing.

To be treated like a possession is wrong. It is also damaging. It deprives an individual of proper self-perception. Because Cain came to see himself as a "thing" rather than a person, he could also see Abel as an object standing in his way, rather than as another human being—and slay him.

עֵשָׂו

ESaV

❦

ESAU

וַיֵּצֵא הָרִאשׁוֹן אַדְמוֹנִי כֻּלּוֹ כְּאַדֶּרֶת שֵׂעָר וַיִּקְרְאוּ שְׁמוֹ עֵשָׂו:

(Vay-yeze ha-rishon admoni kulo ke-aderet se'ar vay-yikre'u shemo Esav)

"And the first came forth ruddy, all over like a hairy mantle; and they called his name Esau."

[Genesis 25:25]

עָשׂוּ (ASU), the same letters as in the Hebrew name עֵשָׂו (ESaV), means finished, done, complete.

Not only did Esau come forth "complete," but that is how he thought of himself. He was already perfect; hence, he had no need to perfect himself. He knew it all; hence, he had not reason to learn any more.

Woe to anyone who thinks he is already perfect. That is the kind of person who is truly finished.

לָבָן

LaVaN

LABAN

Laban, the Haggadah teaches us, was even more dangerous than Pharaoh.

Pharaoh issued a decree

כָּל־הַבֵּן הַיִּלּוֹד הַיְאֹרָה תַּשְׁלִיכֻהוּ

(Kol ha-ben ha-yilod ha-yeorah tashlikhuhu)

"Every son that is born, ye shall cast into the river."
[Exodus 1:22]

We knew where he stood. His wickedness was blatant and open.

לָבָן (LaVaN) means white. On the surface Laban hypocritically offered the image of purity. It was only in retrospect, by reading his name backwards, that we could know that he was actually נָבָל (NaVaL), a reprobate.

Laban kissed Jacob, but it was a kiss of death far more dangerous than the sword of Pharaoh.

פַּרְעֹה

PaROH

PHARAOH

What is the secret of Pharaoh's success? What is the source of his danger to our people?

רַע, the letters resh and ayin that spell the Hebrew word for "evil" (ra), is central to Pharaoh's name. Evil dwelled within him. Yet, surrounding the רַע (ra) on either side is a פ (pe) and a ה (he). It is the power of the mouth, the פֶּה (PeH) to couch evil in such a way that it becomes acceptable.

Hitler in our own days may have been a madman, the personification of evil. Yet his eloquence and his genius at propaganda made him partner with Pharaoh of old. The evildoer becomes truly dangerous when his lips serve the interests of his wicked intent.

עֲמָלֵק

AMaLeK

AMALEKITES

The Amalekites are the archenemy of the Jewish people. For all generations we are commanded:

זָכוֹר אֵת אֲשֶׁר־עָשָׂה לְךָ עֲמָלֵק בַּדֶּרֶךְ בְּצֵאתְכֶם מִמִּצְרָיִם

(Zakhor et asher asah lekha Amalek ba-derekh be-zetkhem mi-Mizrayim)

"Remember what Amalek did unto thee by the way as ye came forth out of Egypt."

[Deuteronomy 25:17]

Many have sought to destroy us. What makes the Amalekites unique? They attacked immediately after the glorious victory of the Jewish people against Egypt at the Red Sea. It was then that the Jews sang the song of praise to God, expressing complete trust and belief.

עֲמָלֵק (AMaLeK) in gematria is ע (ayin) = 70, מ (mem) = 40, ל (lamed) = 30, ק (kof) = 100; total: 240. That is identical to the gematria of the word סָפֵק (SaFeK), doubt: ס (samekh) = 60, פ (fe) = 80, ק (kof) = 100. Amalek cast doubt on the Jews' total trust in God. That is the crime for which the Amalekites must be remembered. That is the sin that must be eradicated before the Messiah will come.

Part VI

Prophecies and Predictions

כִּי לֹא יַעֲשֶׂה אֲדֹנָי יֶהוִֹה
דָּבָר כִּי אִם־גָּלָה סוֹדוֹ
אֶל־עֲבָדָיו הַנְּבִיאִים

(Ki lo ya'aseh Adonay Elohim davar ki im galah sodo
el avadav ha-nevi'im)

עָמוֹס ג:ז

"For the Lord God will do nothing
But He revealeth His counsel
unto His servants the prophets"

Amos 3:7

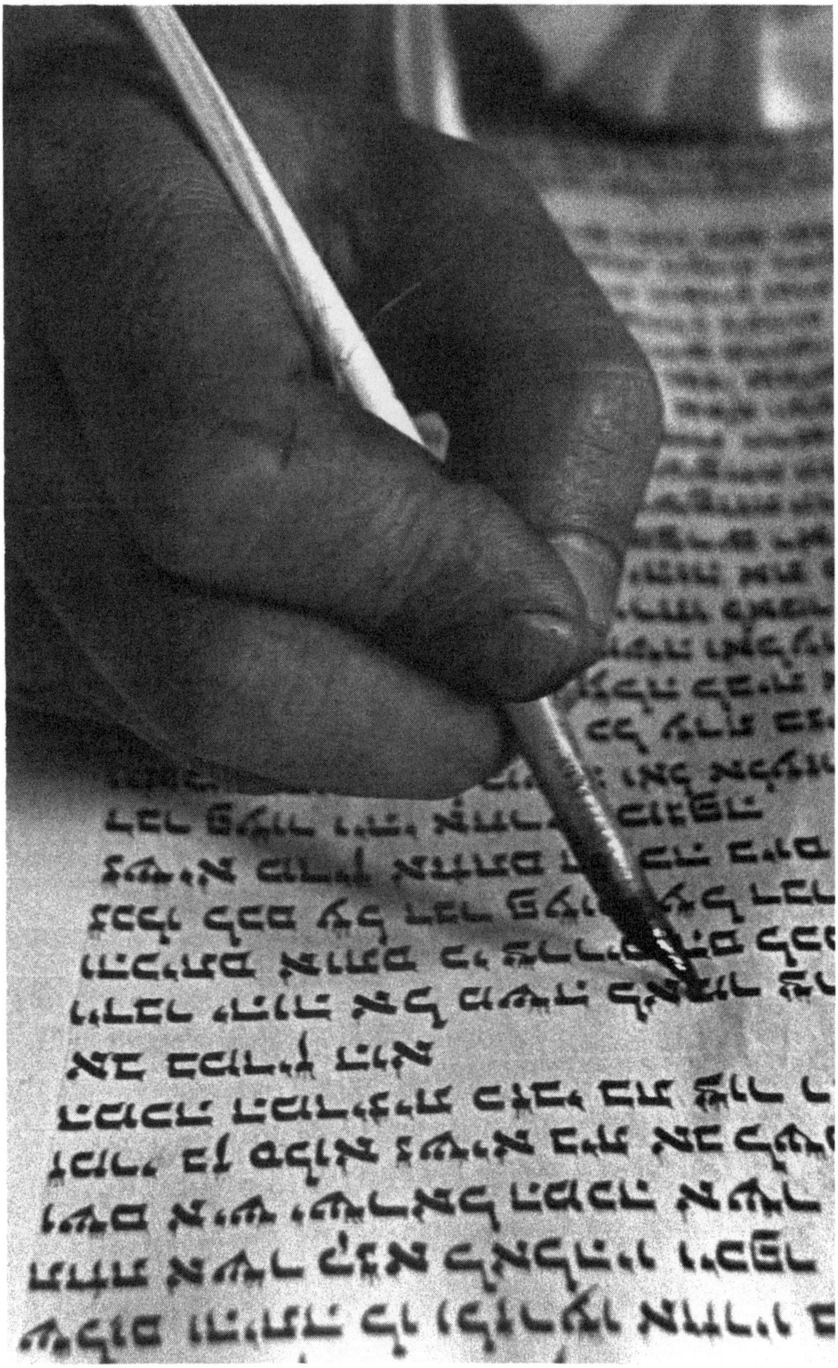

Chapter 19

The Two Temples

AV

THE MONTH OF AB

Both Temples were destroyed on exactly the same day— תִּשְׁעָה בְּאָב (Tish'ah be-Av), the ninth day of the Hebrew month of Av.

The date coincided with an event that had taken place long before, at the time when the Jews in the desert looked forward to entering the Holy Land. They sent forth scouts, or spies, before them. The spies came back with an unfavorable report. They felt that the inhabitants of the land were too strong for them and that the Jews could not possibly capture the land. The people wept and did not have sufficient faith in God. The Almighty said, you cried tonight for no reason; whenever there will be cause for you to weep in years to come, it will occur on this very day of the Ninth of Av.

אָב (AV) means "father." In spite of whatever punishment God administers, remember He is still your *Father* in Heaven.

אָב —there will be destruction of א (alef), the First Temple, and ב (Vet), the Second Temple, on this date.

Rome and Babylonia will be the two nations responsible for the destruction of the House of God. In Hebrew, these two nations respectively begin with the letter א (alef), standing for Edom (Rome), and ב (bet), which stands for Bavel (Babylonia).

וְשָׁכַנְתִּי

Ve-ShaKHaNTiY

AND I SHALL DWELL

The מִשְׁכָּן (MiShKaN), the Sanctuary in the desert, was the prototype for the Temple.

The commandment to build it was given in Exodus 25:8:

וְעָשׂוּ לִי מִקְדָּשׁ וְשָׁכַנְתִּי בְּתוֹכָם

(Ve-asu li mikdash ve-shakhanti be-tokham)

"And let them make Me a sanctuary so that I may dwell amongst them."

Divide the word וְשָׁכַנְתִּי (Ve-ShaKHaNTiY) into two parts and you have a prediction of the number of years the First Temple was to remain standing: וְשָׁכַן (ve-shakhan), and it shall dwell, תִּי (TiY), ת (tav) = 400, י (yod) = 10.

The First Temple lasted exactly 410 years.

וְשָׁכַנְתִּי

Ve-ShaKHaNTiY

AND I SHALL DWELL

The duration of the First Temple is suggested in the word וְשָׁכַנְתִּי (Ve-ShaKHaNTiY), as it was broken down into the parts וְשָׁכַן and תִּי (VeShaKHaN, TiY).

The duration of the Second Temple is also indicated in the same word: in וְשָׁכַנְתִּי (Ve-ShaKHaNTiY) there appears the word וְשֵׁנִי (Ve-SheNiY)—and the second one. What remains are the letters ת (tav), כ (khaf); ת (tav) = 400, כ (khaf) = 20. The Second Temple lasted exactly 420 years.

שְׁלַח
SheLaH

SEND

It was the spies who were responsible for the very first תִּשְׁעָה בְּאָב Tish'ah be-Av of Jewish history.

The Jews in the desert should not have required a scouting party to validate the promise of the Almighty. Since they demanded it, God said unto Moses:

שְׁלַח־לְךָ אֲנָשִׁים וְיָתֻרוּ אֶת־אֶרֶץ כְּנַעַן אֲשֶׁר־אֲנִי נֹתֵן לִבְנֵי יִשְׂרָאֵל

(Shelah lekha anashim ve-yaturu et erez Kena'an asher ani noten li-venei Yisrael)

"Send thou men that they may spy out the land of Canaan which I give unto the Children of Israel."

[Numbers 13:2]

The word שְׁלַח (SheLaH) means to send. It also means to cast out. In the third millennium of world history in the year שלח , שׁ (shin) = 300, ל (lamed) = 30, ח (het) = 8—i.e., in the year 338 B.C.E., the Temple was destroyed, and the Jews were forced into exile for the first time.

Chapter 20

Final Redemption

גּוֹלָה/גְּאוּלָה

GOLaH/GEULaH

EXILE/REDEMPTION

Since the Second Temple was destroyed in 70 C.E., the Jewish people have endured the longest exile of our history.

גּוֹלָה (GOLaH), exile, is our condition until the Messianic era begins. גְּאוּלָה (GEULaH), redemption, is our hope and our ongoing prayer.

What is the difference between גּוֹלָה and גְּאוּלָה, exile and redemption? The letter א (alef). It is the א (alef) of אָנֹכִי (Anokhi), the One representing God, Who must be incorporated into the mentality of the גּוֹלָה (exile) in order to bring about גְּאוּלָה (Redemption).

תָּשֻׁבוּ

TaShuVU

YOU SHALL RETURN

In the days when slavery existed, the Torah decreed that there must come a time when every man goes free. Even those who resold themselves after six years of servitude, and had their ears pierced for voluntary enslavement, could not remain beyond the time of the Jubilee.

וְקִדַּשְׁתֶּם אֵת שְׁנַת הַחֲמִשִּׁים שָׁנָה וּקְרָאתֶם דְּרוֹר בָּאָרֶץ
לְכָל־יֹשְׁבֶיהָ יוֹבֵל הִוא תִּהְיֶה לָכֶם

(Ve-kidashtem et shenat ha-ḥamishim shanah u-keratem deror ba-arez le-khol yoshveha yovel hi tihyeh lakhem)

"And ye shall hallow the fiftieth year and proclaim liberty throughout the land unto all the inhabitants thereof."

[Leviticus 25:10]

These are the words chosen to be inscribed on the Liberty Bell. It is in the Jubilee year that "ye shall return every man unto his possession and ye shall return every man unto his family."

The Hebrew word for "ye shall return," תָּשֻׁבוּ (TaShuVU), seems to be spelled incorrectly. Grammatically it requires another ו (vav). It ought to read תָּשׁוּבוּ (TaShUVU).

Why is it lacking the letter ו (vav), which stands for 6? תָּשֻׁבוּ (without the "vav") is a prediction to the Jewish people of ultimate return to their national homeland. תָּשֻׁבוּ in numbers adds up to 708: ת (tav) = 400, ש (shin) = 300, ב (vet) = 2, ו (vav) = 6. When we write the year, we ignore the millennia. In 1948 on the secular calendar, we witnessed the miracle of Jewish return to Israel. On the Hebrew calendar it was the year 5708. That was the year predicted by the incomplete word תָּשֻׁבוּ (TaShuVU), you shall return. We did return, lacking 6—an all-important 6 million of our people who perished during the Holocaust.

Yet the fulfillment of the prediction of return in precisely that year implied by the gematria of תָּשֻׁבוּ (TaShuVU) gives us firm hope that the words of the Prophets for Final Redemption will come true as well.

Glossary

A	*Alef*	א
AARON	*Aharon*	אהרן
ABRAHAM	*Avraham*	אברהם
ABRAHAM, ISAAC, JACOB	*Avraham, Yizhak, Ya'akov*	אברהם, יצחק, יעקב
ADAM	*Adam*	אדם
ADAM/MAN	*Adam*	אדם
ALL OF ISRAEL	*Kol Yisrael*	כל ישראל
THE ALL-SUFFICIENT ONE	*Shaday*	שדי
AND I SHALL DWELL	*Ve-shakhantiy*	ושכנתי
AND THEY SHALL GIVE	*Ve-natnu*	ונתנו
AND YOU SHALL LOVE	*Ve-ahavta*	ואהבת
BELOVED FRIEND	*Yediyd*	ידיד
BREAD	*Lehem*	לחם
BROTHER	*Ah*	אח
CAIN	*Kayin*	קין
COMMANDMENT	*Mizvah*	מצוה
COVENANT	*Beriyt*	ברית
CROWN	*Keter*	כתר
DAUGHTER	*Bat*	בת
DEATH	*Mavet*	מות
DIED	*Met*	מת
DISCERNMENT	*Biynah*	בינה
ESAU	*Esav*	עשו
EVIL	*Ra*	רע
EXILE/REDEMPTION	*Golah/Geulah*	גולה/גאולה
FALSEHOOD	*Sheker*	שקר
FATHER	*Av*	אב
FIVE	*Hamishah*	חמשה
FRIEND	*Haver*	חבר

GOD	Elohiym	אלהים
GOLD	Zahav	זהב
GRAVE	Kever	קבר
GROUP, CONGREGATION	Zibur	צבור
HAPPINESS	Simhah	שמחה
HE WILL REJOICE	Yismah	ישמח
HEART	Lev	לב
HELPMEET	Ezer	עזר
IN THE BEGINNING	Bereshiyt	בראשית
ISAAC	Yizhak	יצחק
ISRAEL	Yisrael	ישראל
JACOB	Ya'akov	יעקב
JUDAH	Yehudah	יהודה
LABAN	Lavan	לבן
LIFE	Hay	חי
LIFE	Hayyim	חיים
THE LIGHT	Et Ha-or	את־האור
LORD	YHVH (Adonay)	יהוה
LOVE	Ahav	אהב
LOVE	Ahavah	אהבה
LOVE	Hiybah	חיבה
LOVE/FEAR	Ahavah/Yirah	אהבה/יראה
LOVER/ENEMY	Ohev/Oyev	אוהב/אויב
MAN	Iysh	איש
MAN/WOMAN	Iysh/Ishah	איש/אשה
MANKIND	Adam	אדם
MENSTRUATING WOMAN	Niydah	נידה
MESSIAH	Mashiyah	משיח
MONEY	Mamon	ממון
MOSES	Mosheh	משה
MOSES OUR TEACHER	Mosheh Rabeynu	משה רבינו
THE MONTH OF AB	Av	אב
MOTHER	Em	אם
MOURNER	Avel	אבל
NOAH	Noah	נח
ONE	Ehad	אחד

THE ORAL LAW	*Mishnah*	משנה
PEACE	*Shalom*	שלום
PHARAOH	*Paroh*	פרעה
PREGNANCY	*Herayon*	הריון
REJOICED	*Samaḥ*	שמח
THE RIB	*Ha-zela*	הצלע
RIGHTEOUS	*Ẓadiyk*	צדיק
RIGHTEOUS/WICKED	*Ẓadiyk, Rasha*	צדיק/רשע
RUTH	*Rut*	רות
SADNESS	*Ẓarah*	צרה
SEND	*Shelaḥ*	שלח
SON	*Ben*	בן
SOUL	*Neshamah*	נשמה
STRAIGHT/HONEST	*Yashar*	ישר
TORAH	*Torah*	תורה
TRANSGRESSION	*Pesha*	פשע
TRUTH	*Emet*	אמת
UNDERSTANDING	*Sekhel*	שכל
UNJUST GAIN	*Baẓa*	בצע
WAR	*Milḥamah*	מלחמה
WEALTHY MAN	*Ashiyr*	עשיר
WHOLE	*Shalem*	שלם
WICKED PERSON	*Rasha*	רשע
WISDOM	*Ḥokhmah*	חכמה
WOMAN	*Ishah*	אשה
YOU SHALL RETURN	*Tashuvu*	תשבו

Index

Daily bread, 119
Daily prayers, three, 181
Daughter, 164
David, King, 145, 190
Day of Atonement. *See* Yom Kippur
Death, 51–57
   caring for deceased, 63
   mizvot and, 51
   moment of, 128
   not extinction, 125
   proper response to, 57
Decalogue. *See* Ten Commandments
Deceased, caring for, 63
Deliverance, thanks to God for, 50
Desires
   divine will vs., 82
   of sight, 77
   sexual passion, limits to, 166
Died, 53
Discernment, 126
Discipline, need for, 104
Divine law. *See also* Commandments
   purpose of, 85
Dress, 106
Dualism, 24
Duality of Man, 64, 129

Eating blood, 144
Egypt/Egyptians
   exodus from, 161
   idolatries of, 186
   strict justice for, 21
Ehad, 24–25
Elohiym, 20–21
Em, 160–161
Emet, 61–66
End not justify means, 70
Enemy, 100
Esau, 123, 179, 196
Esther, 55
Et Ha-Or, 30
Ethics, 9
Eve, 195. *See also* Adam and Eve
Evil, 79
Exile, 210, 213
   first, 210

redemption, 213
Ezer, 155

Falsehood, 67–72
Family, 159–166
Father, 154–159
Fear, 95
Festival days, 56
First Temple, 207, 208, 209, 210
Five Books of Moses, 34, 85, 99, 188
Forgetfulness, gift of, 86
Forgive and forget, 86
Forgiveness, limits of, 19
Four Matriarchs, 7
Four Sons, 125
Frank, Anne, 147
Free time, too much, 174
Friends, 135–136
   beloved friend, 135
   bride and groom as, 165
   enemy masquerading as, 100
   study partner, 136

Garden of Eden, 82, 86
Garments, 106
Gemara, 66
Geulah, 213
Ghetto, first, 192
Give and take, 96
Giving, 96, 118
   love and, 96
   mizvah of, 118
God, 16–25
   alef, 23
   All Sufficient One, 22
   awareness of, 9
   Ehad, 24–25
   Elohiym, 20–21
   faith in, 35
   male or female, 18
   mercy, 23
   monotheism, 24–25
   One, 23, 24–25
   past, present, and future, 16
   rulership of nations, 21, 25
   Shaday, 22

ABOUT THE AUTHOR

Benjamin Blech has been Rabbi of Young Israel of Oceanside, New York, for over three decades, and is Assistant Professor of Talmud at Yeshiva University in New York City. He has served as Scholar-in-Residence in numerous congregations throughout the United States and Canada, and he has lectured to Jewish communities in Israel, Australia, and many other countries.

Rabbi Blech has written articles for *Tradition, Jewish Life, Reader's Digest, Jewish Week,* and *Newsday.* He is the author of *Understanding Judaism: The Basics of Deed and Creed.*